THE SCORPION'S TAIL

To Zena and my family

The Scorpion's Tail

Antony Sharples

TAPLINGER PUBLISHING COMPANY
NEW YORK

Acknowledgements

Writing this book was the suggestion of my editor, Antony Wood. Several old friends gave me encouragement at the beginning when I had reservations about it, including Nick Waterlow and the amazing Michael Jones. And Lisa Sainsbury gave me the most kind and thoughtful assistance.

First published in the United States in 1976 by
TAPLINGER PUBLISHING CO., INC.
New York, New York 10003

Printed in Great Britain

Library of Congress Catalog Card Number: # 75-26100

ISBN 0-8008-7004-2

Contents

Preface

I was born in 1942 in Lancashire, of what could best be described as bohemian middle-class parentage. My father came originally from the county and was at that time a serving army officer; in peace time he was a professional musician and orchestrator in London. My mother was of Russian parentage. I have one brother, six years older than myself.

Once the bombs had stopped falling the family returned to London, living in Bayswater. In 1948 my parents were divorced. Thereafter my mother, who had apparently never worked, brought us up alone in the slightly unsettled atmosphere of post-war London. I was something of a wayward child, loathing school, preferring from a very early age to find my own activities whenever I could. After attending a number of primary schools, the changes occasioned partly by my mother's relative poverty and consequently frequent housemoving, but more often by my own recalcitrance, I was educated at a London grammar school.

Academically I was an average pupil. I was reasonable at sport, best at cricket. I mixed well with the other boys but tended to be combative or rebellious—I was at home by then, engaging in a struggle with my new stepfather.

I left school at the age of eighteen and became a garage hand. Material aims held little interest for me. I moved through various jobs, idling or living on my wits in between, choosing work with which I did not have to identify.

By 1963 I was a fairly orthodox drop-out. I wrote mediocre poetry, and enjoyed parties, cosmic conversation, heavy drinking and, for some reason, brawling. For what it's worth I was deeply out of sympathy with the aims and ideals of my society, believing it to be afflicted with collective tunnel vision.

This book is not an autobiography or self-portrait, in either intention or form. It is rather an attempt to follow the lines of one set of experiences and some of their implications. I hope that the events described will be read against the background of their period.

London, October 1974

PART ONE

ON THE ROAD

1

The first time I smoked pot was in 1963 when I was twenty. Someone I knew slightly offered me a smoke at a party and I accepted without thinking about the pros and cons; it was there. Before then I hadn't had much interest in drugs at all, insofar as I had ever even been aware of them, and I had no idea of what to expect.

It was no fun really; I felt dazed and not quite in command but the feeling wasn't pleasurable. I decided it was a waste of time, a nothing kick, and went off to get some sleep. But a few connections had been activated and when it turned up again, a few weeks later, I tried it once more and got stoned.

It was all rather self-conscious that time: we sat quietly—on the floor of course—with records playing in the background while the Man with the marijuana juggled with cigarette papers and filter tips and passed the joints round as he made them. It was a very warm, innocent sort of high, the giggly sort—people shouting with laughter at the tiniest provocation, conversations turning into harmless nonsense.

But it opened certain doors; there were hints of other directions that could be followed up, areas outside my previous experience where the normal rules of perception didn't operate. After a couple of months of smoking now and then I found it easy to convince myself that this was something worth exploring. In my own way I was into 'kicks', into trying as many different things as possible.

I was into a lot of funny things . . . but not, apparently, common sense. So when, a few months after my first smoke, I was asked if I wanted to smuggle some, naturally I said yes.

The idea was laid on me by a friend whom I hadn't seen for over a year. His name was Gerry and when I first knew him he was an actor, had been since he was ten years of age. Gerry was a thin, edgy Jewish guy with a tee-shirt-and-jeans juvenile delinquent look, very talented, very successful. But he had tired of the stage and had left it a couple of years before, turning to hustling in the show-business field. I'd had a few letters from him and I knew that he had collected a cabaret troupe together to tour the Middle East and had been doing very well. That was the last I'd heard.

Then I came back to my place one evening and found him waiting on the doorstep. He didn't look too good, his clothes were dirty and he was obviously dead tired. It turned out he'd just hitch-hiked all the way from Tangier, three days solid. I took him inside and he told me the news over a drink. Dog eat dog. They were doing gigs in Beirut when their promoter, a London club owner, had turned them over for all they had, just before pay day with a lot of back wages owing.

The promoter had vanished and Gerry had lost his share of the profits. But it seemed that there had been just enough money to get Gerry and his girlfriend onto a plane and away to Tangier. What had happened to the other girls in the troupe? He wasn't sure. Did they have access to any bread at all? He rather thought not. He could hardly look after them all even if he was their manager. Besides, that was in the past; he thought he had found a way of making some money in Tangier. Did I have anything to do with pot these days? And he pulled out a walletful of Tangier weed. We settled down to a smoke. The girls were forgotten, their subsequent fate a mystery.

There were twelve kilos of the stuff waiting in Morocco with his girlfriend as security for payment. He'd bought it up in the mountains, far away from the gangsters and informers in Tangier, and it was dirt cheap. If he could raise some money in London he could retrieve both girl and dope—and he had a car to run it in. Did I want to come back with him and run it up to Scandinavia where the Customs were easier? I was welcome, I'd make some money and I could get stoned all the time.

I said I would help at this end: Morocco was too far. Besides he was in a hurry and it would take me a few days to get things together. We worked something out. Gerry could get straight back to Morocco, organize the stuff as far as the Scandinavian Customs and I could meet him when he brought his lady back to London. He thought he could cover petrol costs by taking some English people from Tangier to Denmark or Sweden—they might even help get the gear through Customs—the pot was good quality and there were apparently plenty of users in Sweden. The risks wouldn't be great.

He'd picked the right person from his point of view. I didn't own any of the stuff and didn't really want to make any money except to cover myself. I was simple enough to go along for the ride and the experience. Dealing seemed exciting and the idea of infinite supplies of weed beautiful. I didn't care what Gerry got out of it—it was his scene and if he got it to Sweden he'd have done most of the work. Gerry was a breadhead, about the hardest and fastest hustler I had ever met, and I had no illusions about his motives; but we had known each other a while and, on the whole, trusted each other. Since he'd started smoking he seemed to have become a bit more human and he wanted to enjoy the trip as well as make some money. I was the only person mental enough to want to enjoy it with him.

He left later that day and we arranged it so that I would have at least a day's notice of his return. Of course I wasn't sure if he'd make it without getting busted, so I raised what money I could without burning anything down, just in case. Then I waited to see if he scored. Within a week I had a cable telling me things were working and when he was due back; two days after that he was at my place again, successful, and we were ready to go. I told the landlady I had to go away and not to destroy my belongings if she didn't hear from me, packed a couple of cases, picked up a new passport and split. I thought I had nothing to lose anyway.

The gear was already in Stockholm. They had packed it around the bodywork of the car and stuffed the spare wheel solid—in those days one could get away with relatively unsophisticated tricks like that—and there had been no trouble at the frontiers. Gerry had stayed in the capital just long enough to confirm that there was a market and to unload the stuff. Leaving it there was risky—anyone cool enough to look after nearly thirty-pounds weight of grass was also likely to be sharp enough to vanish with it—but Gerry had found a fifteen-year-old girl who seemed fairly innocent. And she had a safe place for stashing it. All we had to to do was get rid of it when we arrived.

I got this from Gerry while we were driving to Dover to pick up the night ferry. With all the gear up North we wanted to get there as quickly as possible and we drove flat out after Dunkirk, sleeping in snatches in the car, staying briefly in a German motel and reaching Denmark in fast time. We took the short ferry at Helsingborg and drove from there, across Sweden, to the capital.

The atmosphere hit me. This was in January, right in the middle of the long Swedish winter and I loved it—the land, the snow, the very short, very sunny days. Christmas card stuff, complete with rolling pine forests all the way and dozens of huge, frozen, sheet-white lakes. The country was shrouded, shrouded in snow, shrouded under trees and—for eighteen hours of the day—shrouded in darkness: nothing menacing, but always a sense of something hidden, something held back.

And Stockholm was worthwhile, when we reached it, sitting, or rather floating, on water. The Swedes were busy knocking it down and building flyovers at the time but they'd left the old town alone, my favourite part, a warren of alleys and old town houses leading up to the palace.

We arrived in the morning, took a sleep in the car and then started looking for the girl with the weed. We tracked her down to one of the old town cafés and hustled her into the car to take us to the gear. Where was it? The kid, a lovely and precocious schoolgirl, told us it was in 'that safe place'. It would only take two minutes to get there, to the central bank.

'In the bank?' I asked, incredulous. 'What do you mean in the bank?'

'Oh, it's all right. It's in the vaults. Where else would I put it?'

She had a lot of front, that girl, for a fifteen-year-old and I still don't know what she told them in the bank. We were a bit uncertain about it all. One just didn't deposit cannabis in central banks. Still, we drove over there, pulled up outside and walked in, a little nervously—and the smell hit me like a hammer before I was through the swing doors.

It was ridiculous, the whole bank reeked of the stuff and it wasn't the sort of smell people would usually ignore; after all it had only recently come out of the ground and was sweating like silage. I began to get the horrors and slid behind a marble pillar while the chick went bouncily to withdraw her deposit. Gerry stared at the floor, frowning. But disaster didn't come. And the deputy manager who brought up carrier bag after carrier bag of—almost steaming—marijuana went on chatting away to the girl with a smile on his face. I was glad to get out, though.

With the stuff safely in the car boot we could have a decent rest, and the girl took us back to her place to straighten out and stay for the night. Her place was a flat in her parents' house which she shared with her sister, seeing the parents about three times a day. No-one would object to our staying, nobody would dare to ask if there was anyone in the flat. Swedish parents were into teenage liberation. We were left alone and lazed about there until the evening, recovering from the journey. Some of the kid's friends called in that night while we were stretching out and somebody mentioned pot. The evil Englishmen produced the carrier bags and turned them on. They nearly mobbed us: there was a pot famine on and they'd been waiting for some to arrive for weeks. We were in.

It was a funny smoking scene in Stockholm. In 1964 smoking was confined to a minority in London, a few 'heads' and the show-business and arts network. In Stockholm it seemed to be the main kick for a lot of the young people, mostly educated middle class kids; there wasn't much show-business anyway so smoking got spread about, not only in the users' homes but in the universities and high schools.

But the way they smoked was a bit unpotlike: they took it like their parents—whom they affected to despise—took aquavit. They enjoyed it, but rather frantically, and I rarely felt relaxed when smoking with them. Swedish heads like speed and the whole upside-downer madness trip that goes with it. They couldn't get speed then; there was never enough preludin, a speed-type pill, so they took pot and took it in a very speedy way.

But selling it was fun. After taking it easy that first night we started out the next afternoon in the coffee bars and restaurants, lining up connections for later in the day when more people would be around. That evening we did the first deal in the simplest possible way: went down to a club, picked up a couple of girls to dance with and offered them a smoke. They were hip and we went back to their flat, got stoned together and sold them a few pounds' worth. Business and pleasure together. The girls were very approachable, especially if you were a foreigner, and they always had money, or at least a boyfriend who would produce it. That seemed to be the main function of most of the boyfriends I met.

We fell into a routine very quickly. Mornings were for resting or for finding out where we'd woken up. Come the afternoon we'd call on people at their homes to see what they wanted and to fix up any larger deals which took more time and negotiation than casual meets in clubs. After that we made it to the old town where there were a few jazz clubs or discotheques frequented by smokers; there would usually be a small crowd waiting for us and we'd take some of them away to do the deals.

It was safer to work it from other people's places rather than from the hotel we'd moved into; the sort of groups we gathered would have got any hotel busted on suspicion and anyway it was nice moving from place to place. Pot must have been very short before we arrived because we were about the most spoiled Englishmen who ever arrived in Stockholm: just about anything we wanted was ours in return for grass.

Selling weed used to be considered a warmer thing than dealing junk or speed; so people were friendly and didn't get paranoid with us or resentful of the money flowing all one way. Not that we made much money the first week because we were so disorganized from smoking stuff ourselves, all the time. I found out then the more you smoke the less you need—nice—and one puff on a joint in the morning used to get me heavily stoned for the next three or four hours. So, although we thought of ourselves as rather clever and businesslike, a lot of the time we just didn't get it together at all. We lost addresses, we forgot who we were meeting, couldn't remember the exchange rate or what money we'd been given. And we never quite knew where we'd end up after a day of dealing. There were strange, mysterious trips to the country—the addresses probably given to us the same morning—where we'd meet more of the rich Stockholm hipsters. They weren't usually much good at business after a smoke either; so simple negotiations dragged on through the hours over endless cups of tea and cream cakes. Both sides usually lost track after a while and took snap decisions out of tiredness or intoxication. They usually bought in the end, the quality of the stuff saw to that.

We threw a party in the country. We had the weed stashed with an American called Steve, a sort of pre-hippy, who was looking after a country house while the owner—whom Steve was obviously hustling—was away. The remaining gear was still on the bush and had to be sieved and refined; so we got some Stockholm girls together and invited them out for a threshing party. It turned into a gay time, for the pot dusted as we 'worked' and gradually covered the place, the phones, bookshelves, even the fridge, with fine, grey-green pollen. The girls made tea with it, they baked a cake with it, they put it between bits of bread. Everyone was slightly hysterical at being, literally, drenched in the stuff.

The correct Swedish note was introduced by the unannounced arrival of the owner. A middle-aged, straight-looking fellow with a goatee, he stood there in his snowy raincoat, staring, silent, rigid. Everyone ignored him except Steve and myself—and Steve started running around trying to explain things, picking up and straightening the odd cushion, trying to save the situation. Looking at the man's house, the bushes and stalks covering the carpet, the half-dressed girls still cavorting, the polythene bags full of refined gear, I decided you couldn't explain this one away, ever, and offered him a smoke outright, before he could get his bearings and before Steve, who'd assured us his 'friend' was four hundred miles away, could wreck things totally.

He was so utterly stunned (I was digging his face, he kept doing little double-takes, looking for things he knew, trying to make sure he really lived there) that he accepted—and lost all the initiative. He dragged on the spliff I thrust under his nose, forgot all the appalling things we were doing with his house and started arguing with the American. While they were at it we cleared up, keeping him away from the phone. But it was all right, he actually began to like us. Later on, when Steve refused to stay with him, he asked us to take him into Stockholm with us and we packed him into the back of the car with three others. Weird. . . . From a carrier bag he produced a huge rubber torch which he kept shining onto the girls' legs, in spite of protests. He'd put it away and then startle us all with the light again, as though checking something. We dropped him at a hotel and left him to think it was all imagination.

Offering gear to strangers, especially older strangers, was dangerous but I did it once more, a few days after our harvest festival. We got stuck in a blizzard one night without enough petrol to get us anywhere useful and Gerry, losing patience, simply ran the car into someone's garage. We piled sacks and newspapers all over the vehicle, dug out all the clothes we could find and tried to sleep. In the morning there was another surprised Swede: we leered at him as he threw back the doors, blowing smoke, uncaring and cold. He was cool enough to offer us breakfast before asking for explanations and we walked up the drive, shivering, to his large and empty country house.

A sad morning. He had been one of the country's leading opera singers but his career had ended abruptly after some unnamed disaster which had damaged his brain. Over breakfast he started to talk about suicide. Again! At eight in the morning they talked about suicide! We were the first visitors he had faced in months. I tired of more Swedish melancholy; compassion got the better of discretion and I gave him a smoke.

That did the trick, cheered him up for a time and he became quite expansive, even laughed a little. When it was time to leave he was down again, though, and he asked us to come and stay whenever we wanted. What could you do? He was standing at the door as we drove off, in front of that lovely house, in the snow, quite alone.

We decided we needed a break. We'd been hustling for two weeks by now and something over half the grass was sold, but the pace had been hectic. We thought a few days away from Stockholm would do us good; we would smoke less for a while and let things cool down in the capital before we became too well known. We knew of a connection in Gothenburg, in the South, who we understood would take a very large deal; so we decided to make the trip down there, take it easy, have a rest.

Gothenburg was a quiet city, very businesslike and mercantile with none of the Stockholm flash. We arrived in the early morning with the sun shining down over the harbour, the sea a deep, cold blue, and we began to feel clean and healthy again. We found the address we wanted quickly enough, a big eighteenth-century town house overlooking the quays, but we couldn't find a way into the place. We circled around looking for a tradesmen's entrance (!) and calling up to the windows until finally a scruffy-looking little guy came down and let us into a side door. He was Stig, our main contact, and he kept pulling at his chin and giggling, stoned solid before we'd even arrived. He took us up six flights of cold stairs and explained the scene.

I suppose they would be called squatters now. The huge house where I'd thought to spend a gracious weekend had been the municipal old people's home and was due to be demolished later in the year. For the present there were six or seven heads living there, and the authorities seemed to be ignoring them. We were introduced and some grass was passed round but the atmosphere was curious. They had the whole of the top floor of the building, a tiny corner of which had been partitioned into bedrooms; there was almost no furniture and very little light—the curtains remained drawn the whole time we were there. There were no clocks.

The two main features of the place were a stage and a thirty-foot rack of theatrical costumes; this had been the home's theatre. Logically, I guess, the heads tended to wear the costumes, which ones depending on their mood and how stoned they were.

That evening I lay on a mattress in a candlelit corner while people floated about the place like moths, now trying, now discarding, period dress and eighteenth-century boots and spurs. I stared, dumbly, and accepted the joints that were passed over, wondering how I'd slipped into this one.

For four days we tried to sell that batch of grass. But the atmosphere of the place was pure madness; nothing could be done, we were drawn into the whole fantasy. None of the residents went out of the house while we were there; the only contact with the outside world was one little bearded man who would come in with breakfast on his way to work, telling us what time—and what day—it was. He had the same problem as we did, though. Each morning he decided to have just one joint before work. Every time he got hung up. About midnight he'd pull himself together and stagger home, warning us he'd only see us for a few minutes the next morning; when he returned the whole cycle would start all over again. Still, he got the breakfast organized, the household sitting round a forty-foot oak table in the kitchen, naked. It was usually the main meal of the day, hippy-type food, vegetarian stuff or porridgy things: I copped out on that one and got our working man to bring me in smorgasbord. I was wasting away.

Now and then we'd bring up the question of a sale. We'd wait till the time was right and some of the people weren't too stoned and we'd corner them. But no, somebody would suggest cleaning the windows or chopping wood and they'd be away again, quite out of reach, often getting us to join in. No way.

On the fourth day we got hip and hid all the grass. Then we sat around, scratching, waiting for them to come down: no more samples till we got something sorted out. Samples? Those lunatics must have smoked a quarter-pound of gear since we'd arrived, as well as everything they'd had of their own. Gradually they got the message and began to congregate around us wondering how to deal with this unwelcome intrusion from the hard world outside. Once they realized what was happening, though, they hustled like madmen, sending one of the girls out—actually out of the pad—to raise extra money from friends. By lunchtime they'd bought the lot and we could all relax again. Funny, money was no problem at all for our squatters.

By then all we wanted to do was get back to sober old Stockholm. They honoured us by drawing the curtains and waving goodbye from the windows, one or two of them tearful, all begging us to return soon, preferably with more pot. I didn't want to go through that number again, though.

We had a couple more large customers lined up in Stockholm: and if they bought that meant the bulk of the weed would be gone. We could knock the rest out without sweating or taking chances. There was a temptation to get more. Turkey was Gerry's preference rather than risking the North African Customs again so soon; and in Turkey it would be block hashish rather than grass, easier to smuggle, easier to sell. On the drive back to Stockholm we considered a few of the difficulties and sketched out a plan; assuming the price was right in Turkey we were sure it could be done.

But back in the big city we found the talk was all of speed;

there was a shortage of preludin and people, having heard of us, began asking us if we could do anything about it. They were mainly Gerry's contacts, not mine; I'd never had much to do with speed-type drugs and didn't like speedfreaks much. Preludin wasn't actually amphetamine-based but very similar in its effect: the Swedish users did all the usual methedrine-like things, talking all the time, nervy, jumping about, getting hung up on cleaning their shoes or making incredible little drawings on table napkins. They had trouble with their eyes, too, and developed a fixed, eye-popping stare. I tended to avoid them. Most of the ones who asked us to deal were too unreliable and disorganized to get the money together, anyway, and even Gerry wasn't very interested; it was all too uncertain.

Then a girl I knew, tall Vera, who dug back massage, asked us both to meet a friend of hers for dinner. Lars was a sculptor and designer and lived in a fine, modern little house by one of the Stockholm inlets, surrounded by trees with a flyover a hundred metres away. He met us at the door, very tall, very thin, about thirty, with swept-back hair and a long-drawn, bony face; he had beautiful long fingers which he waved as he showed us his collections. But I was digging his wide, popping eyes.

We talked politely through the meal. He knew of us by reputation and Vera, being a bit melodramatic, had maybe made us out to be harder than we were; in any case he seemed to be scared of us at first. But after the food he relaxed and opened out. I rolled a joint and offered him a smoke. He declined. Would we like some pills? No thanks. Did we mind if he took some? Go ahead. He started rooting around underneath the graph paper and art magazines until he found some preludin tubes, some old bottles and instruments—and a big syringe.

I said: 'You inject those things? They're bloody slimming pills, man, you surely can't fix those?'

'Oh, yes, always,' Vera broke in, 'it is much better that way, much stronger.'

She was digging the whole thing and I gave her a warning look to shut up; I could do without her expert knowledge just now. For some reason I felt annoyed and disturbed at Lars fixing the pills; the whole thing seemed to be getting too serious, too heavy, far away from the happy smoking buzz.

But Lars wasn't arguing and calmly went on with his work, crushing up the pills, mixing them with water and filtering the binder out through cotton wool.

'All the impurities are removed, you see,' he said dreamily to no-one in particular.

I shrugged my shoulders, rolled up another joint and sat watching, moodily. He didn't put it straight into the vein but made a long issue out of shooting it into the muscle, probing around, the centre of attention in the spotlit room. It was a strange, strange sight and one that didn't relate at all to anything I'd ever seen before—as though at a dinner party the host had suddenly started cutting off his own head, without comment. And it was physically, directly unpleasant. For a moment my head swam.

There wasn't much change in him. His voice dropped and he looked even more cadaverous than before, but nothing more. He'd crushed up about half a dozen tablets and now he sat there, fiddling around with water and tissues, cleaning his little mortar and pestle, quite happy. I looked at the others. Vera was stoned, staring into space; Gerry, as usual, quite expressionless, hidden behind shades. Was it only me that found it weird? I wanted to leave.

The host's voice seemed to come from a long way away. Could we get him some more tablets from England or Germany? There were none around, he needed them to work, he was willing to pay the right price. So the lovely Vera had been the honest broker. At least this was concrete, unlike the looners who'd asked us before. I was uncertain. Gerry lifted his head slightly. If it was a large enough quantity, he said, perhaps it would make sense, but for one person. . . .

'That's all right,' said Lars, 'I have friends, some of them professional. It would be worthwhile.'

But I wanted to get away and we agreed to meet the next day; I was dead tired all of a sudden. Drifting off to sleep at Vera's I thought about it. The pot would soon be gone; a little trip to London, help the man out, some money to get to Turkey with. What else did I think of? I don't remember. Anyway I fell asleep.

The next day we met Lars and one of his friends at the Golden Circle restaurant. The friend owned jewellers' shops in the better part of Stockholm but they seemed to be a cover for his hustling. I didn't take to him very much; he was a big, blond, German-looking guy in a leather jacket and he made me uneasy; he came out with edgy, heavy vibrations. He didn't give much away; said he could handle a moderate amount of preludin straight off, a few hundred pounds worth, and more later. If we could get more weed he'd handle that too, and he even had friends who might take heroin and cocaine. He was a busy man.

I went downstairs to ring Vera and find out what she knew about the friend, Carl I think his name was. She told me he was solid; he might not be a charmer but he had plenty of money and she'd never heard of him turning anyone over or letting them down. Besides he was a friend of Lars whom she'd known and trusted for years. I went back inside thinking cynically that Vera's judgement wasn't the best I could depend on.

When I joined the others it was clear Gerry wanted to go ahead. For my part I sat there without saying much for a few minutes and then said yes, I'd come in for a little piece of the action, say a thousand or two thousand pills, a couple of hundred pounds. Then I sat back again and listened to the band, following the conversation with one half of my head and dragging on an inconspicuous joint. The whole scene depressed me. I was repelled by Lars and his petty, second-rate fixing habit; I distrusted the blond number in the leather jacket. So I wanted the excitement of smuggling and dealing, but doing things with breadheads like this—I might as well have taken a job in the city and sold something legal.

Before we shook hands on a deal the heroin and cocaine were mentioned again. Carl thought he could handle it but wasn't certain about details; Gerry thought he could get it but didn't know if he wanted to. Both were ambivalent, both attracted by the enormous prices people were willing to pay. In the end it was left open. We were leaving for London next day or the day after and we expected to be back in a week to ten days.

Gerry drove me back to Vera's, neither of us saying very much. In the streetlights I could see his face was set and tight the way it was when he was concentrating on a project; the wheels were whirring away. It was snowing hard outside again, clogging the windscreen-wipers. I asked him about the H and C, was he interested? He wasn't sure, and made a face; it was like signing someone's death warrant, he said.

'Sure,' I said, and unwisely, 'but you could probably get used to it.'

'Meaning *you* couldn't?'

'I didn't say that. I just can't see the point there. I don't want bread that much.'

'You're going to buy preludin, is that so different then? At least with junk you aren't shooting chalk into your veins.'

'—'

'Because,' he said, 'you've always got answers when you do things—you bend things to fit what you want to do. Before you said you didn't want to make any money, that you dug the subversion; now you're selling pills. And you don't like selling junk, you think you're above it and maybe I'm not; but next week or next year you'll have good reasons for selling that. too. Moral ones, man.'

'When did I ever come out with moral reasons for anything, Gerry?'

'I don't remember,' he said, 'it's your attitude.'

I said we were both tired and stoned and to leave it out, talk another time. He was hung up with his own uncertainties about junk and all the heaviness that went with it, ten-year sentences, guns, conscience, the lot. Maybe he was right about me and my attitudes; I didn't know.

We parted on good terms, he drove off to his chick and I went upstairs to Vera, the massage queen.

Two days later we were in London, leaving the car at Dunkirk and taking the train into town. Gerry had all the West End friends and contacts and he went off to line them up while I hustled up a few pounds to pay for the pills. We gave ourselves till Sunday to get the thing together and leave again—four days.

The pill market was concentrated in Soho. I spent one afternoon with Gerry in Berwick Street meeting some of the dealers and finding out what went on. It was all very well organized, unlike the pot business; instead of travellers bringing in the gear and hoping to find a market it was down to professional crooks, with regular sources of supply, fixed prices and no getting stoned on the job. All the pills, preludin, dexedrine, purple hearts, came through the same channels, knocked off in transit to the chemist's either by regular pilfering or by the outright hijacking of the delivery van. The drugs were on the street within forty-eight hours of the theft.

The first dealer I spoke to was standing under a lamp-post listening to a miniature transistor radio hanging from his wrist. An absurd figure in camel hair coat and sharp hat, he told us—yes, out of the side of his mouth—that he could do a few thousand at sixpence each: not before Saturday though, there was a bit of a shortage and they'd have to be stolen specially for us. We said yes.

Gerry then decided to do the heroin and cocaine. One of his contacts had friends with prescription junk and he agreed to ask them to sell to Gerry. But the contact, a cockney called Geoff, had more to offer than that. He'd been hanging around the West End since he was fifteen, knew what it was all about, and had had a small junk habit himself. Having been imprisoned for possession, he'd absconded and was now on the run; in return for a free passage and some cash he was willing to carry the stuff through Customs and act as a general runner. Geoff was all right. I liked him and he seemed reliable. At first sight he looked like a builder's labourer but the eyes gave it away, always fixed on some strange goal of his own, blue and distant. He sensed that he was going to start fixing again if he stayed in London; perhaps he sensed that he would anyway. He was cool but without hope.

They collected the stuff from the junkies on the Friday night when the next week's prescriptions were picked up from Boots in Piccadilly. The heroin came in tiny hypodermic tablets, the cocaine in fluffy crystals. Both were measured and sold by the grain, units of sixty milligrammes; Gerry bought fifty of each at ten shillings a grain. The next night we drove around picking up the preludin. There were hang-ups, people getting delayed, stuff not turning up, one of the boys trying to rob us—for our dealer had had to subcontract and get the pills from other people as well as from his own sources. We finished up, done in, at seven in the morning and left England later the same day.

There were four of us now, for Gerry's 'wife' was coming with us, thinking correctly that she might never see him again if she stayed in London. Having been a Middle Eastern dancer, Pat was stripping again, a well-built blonde lady from Leeds with dreams of settling down to steady clubwork, commuting from a freehold in Finsbury Park.

Before we left I was talking with a friend of mine, a boy I had known when he was at Oxford, drunken and irresponsible. Now our paths were drawing apart as he settled down. He was at a loss.

'But why? And why with them of all people?'

'Why judge?' I answered. 'They're all right.'

'Dirt and darkness,' said Victor, who knew me, 'you have a weakness for dirt and darkness.'

We drove slowly, stayed in hotels, dropped pills and played word games, invented by Pat. The only dangerous frontier we had to face was at Flensburg on the German-Danish border. We had a polythene vest for Geoff to wear, beautifully stitched into compartments by the versatile Pat; it held all the junk, all the pills, snugly and without bulging. It looked rather like a flak-jacket, which in a sense it was. The plan was for Geoff to have the stuff stashed away in it and pass through the Customs as a hitch-hiker. He looked quite respectable and had extra cash on him so they wouldn't think he was a vagrant. He also possessed a brand new visitor's passport, full of lies. He was to go on ahead and we would pick him up on the other side. Altogether rather a good, cowardly plan. It might have been even safer if we had crossed the frontier first; this way we wouldn't know if he had made it or not until we were at the Customs ourselves and we could easily be tied in with him. But this was Gerry's idea: without us behind him friend Geoff might just possibly vanish into the North German plain with all the merchandise. Gerry had a head for details.

A couple of miles from Flensburg we pulled off the road and drove down dirt tracks until we found a quiet clearing in the forest. We went over Geoff's cover story with him and started rigging him up in his vest. There was no real contingency plan—except that if Geoff was searched Gerry and I didn't intend to stop voluntarily, that was understood.

Geoff was the one at risk but all of us were nervous as we buried the packages, bottles and other incriminating odds and ends. My own nervousness had a pleasurable edge to it which got me. This part of things felt clean compared to the buying and selling of the gear, clean and sharp even to the surroundings, the trees, the birds in the clearing, the sound of the cars far back on the main road. It was another kind of high and I sat on a tree stump digging it all, in the sun.

Then I looked at Geoff, strapped into his vestful of mischief and began to laugh. The pills made him look like a pearly king from Lambeth, not a smuggler. We helped him on with his shirt and jacket, drove him back to the road and wished him luck, dropping him off about four hundred metres from the frontier.

And it was a walkover. After waiting twenty minutes or so we followed on and arrived at the post as he was leaving the other side, a free man. They checked us over briefly, asked why we were back so soon and what our plans were and waved us through. We said thank you, goodbye, and picked up Geoff around the first bend in the road.

We had a little celebration later that afternoon on the ferry crossing the bight, eating well and getting slightly drunk with the happy Danes. In the middle of it I felt strange and went up on deck to get away from the others. I smoked a little joint, staring at the hard blue northern sea again, looking at the snow in the distance and thinking. The conversation with Victor came back to me and I wondered about things and about darkness, probably drunk. I felt, suddenly, that I was quite out on my own, apart from the others downstairs, apart from everyone back in England, quite alone. I chucked the joint away and went into the bar; it was getting cold and the sun was going down.

There wasn't much we could do in Stockholm the first couple of days, both Carl and Lars were out of town and we didn't fancy trying to sell this brand on the streets. The others moved into a hotel; I went back to stay with Vera and passed the time seeing some of the Stockholm faces or sitting in the Golden Circle listening to jazz.

I spent part of an evening with American Steve; he'd moved back to his 'friend' in the country. It was still weird. He never used the front door of the house, access was by a rustic wooden ladder up to a window, the ladder being hauled up every night. The Swede didn't show; for all I knew he was under the floorboards holding his torch in his hand. In any case Steve had moved in some sort of girlfriend, a novelist from Amsterdam who wore jackboots and glared at me when I joked about Dutch dykes. She bought him a clean shirt.

I wasn't so full of grass this time around but I started dropping the preludin now and then; in a restaurant one evening I found myself drawing strange little pictures on the tablecloth. I eased off the next morning but their effect probably contributed to the atmosphere of paranoia that overcame us like a cloud. First off, the police intercepted some drugs at the frontier. They then decided to purge Stockholm, thinking that the smugglers were in town; suddenly there seemed to be police everywhere we went, asking about stuff and pulling in suspected users. It didn't help that the people they were looking for were also foreigners, or believed to be; wires got crossed and they began to ask about us, ironically, as we had nothing to do with that deal at all.

The unpleasantness came to a head with the arrival of the police at the hotel. They couldn't have had much to go on because, finding that Gerry and Co. were out, they just had a quick look over the rooms and left a message that they'd be coming back. But that was enough for Gerry. He wanted to leave for Turkey immediately before they could question him; just answering routine inquiries would put him on the spot: like, what exactly had he been doing on his last visit here? I agreed that it was best to go as soon as we could see Carl and get rid of the pills.

When I finally got hold of him he said he had the horrors too, and thought the police might be getting close to us. I tried to reassure him and he eventually agreed to meet us that evening. Something about his manner on the phone made me even more uneasy than I had been before.

'Have you any problems?' I asked.

He hesitated only a moment. 'Things are very difficult at present. Money is tight, my friend.'

(Well, well!)

'All right, tell me what you want to say, Carl.'

And out it came. He could only pay seventy-five per pill instead of a hundred. I mentioned something about an agreed deal. Well, yes, but things had changed hadn't they? Did I still want to sell to him? There wasn't much to say to that: he knew I did. I rang off and turned to Gerry.

'Well,' I said, 'you heard that. I told you he was a cunt from the word go; I think he set this up.'

Gerry calmed me down. We had to use him now. With Lars still out of town we couldn't start looking for new dealers, it was just too dangerous. We had to go and play it by ear, see what we could salvage.

We drove over and parked the car away from the shop where it wouldn't be seen. Carl was waiting inside; he let us in quickly and drew all the blinds. It was attractive in a flash sort of way, deep green carpets, modern paintings and antique swords on the walls. There were a very few display cabinets full of goldwork placed here and there.

Carl didn't present such a pretty picture. He was even speedier than usual and was sweating a lot; while Gerry and I sat down at the back of the shop he paced around, frowning to himself, talking in his unfriendly way—and carrying a huge pair of scissors that he wouldn't put down. I began to get my sense of humour back; this was familiar ground: craziness again.

He and Gerry haggled over the heroin and coke while I sat back and dug the sight of them hustling each other. Carl kept reminding Gerry that it was dangerous to hang onto the stuff with the present police aggravation, Gerry pointing out that it was easy to conceal and, unlike the preludin, easy to sell outside Sweden. They couldn't agree and in the end Carl bought a small amount as samples. I must say it was some fantastic price that Gerry was asking, about a thousand pounds for the gear that had cost him fifty. I nearly fell off my chair when I heard it. How could he keep a straight face?

If Gerry was disappointed in Carl he didn't show it. We had a cup of coffee (we made it while the maniac strode up and down with his scissors), and Carl let him look at some of the gold bracelets while we argued about the preludin.

In the end we reached a thieves' compromise: Carl agreed to pay slightly more than he'd said on the phone—and I lifted one of the packets while he was trying to watch Gerry and the gold bracelets. That meant we came out roughly where we had originally agreed; Lars could have the surplus when I saw him. He took the stuff away and brought me my money—discarding the scissors as he did so and taking down one of the swords! He stood by me as I pocketed the bread, slapping his leg with the sabre.

'I still think you acted rather badly, you know,' I told him reproachfully.

The sword swished foolishly.

'Well I'm sorry. But in this country business is business. Yes?'

He was wrong there. Sweden was one place where business was never just business.

2

We drove across Europe and towards Turkey. With the Swedish paranoia behind us we were glad to take our time, stopping frequently in the cities, spending money—and dipping frequently into the drug supply.

Having junk—heroin and cocaine—alongside the pills and marijuana inevitably made us less conscious of the gulf between it and all other drugs. There, in the car, it was just another variant, another form of merchandise, more risky certainly but familiar and available. There were no skull and crossbones signs on the bottles.

And the rather frightening image I, at least, had built up of junk-taking—medical apparatus, tying up veins, blood and accidents, something totally *other*—was attenuated when I discovered that one could take it without a syringe. It could be 'snorted'—sniffed into the nostrils and absorbent mucous membranes through a rolled up paper tube. Snorting was less addictive, Geoff told me, and much less dangerous than fixing.

The transition was hardly noticeable. . . . Later, back in England when I took my first *injection* of heroin, I was aware of a sharp break, a moment when things had changed decisively and for ever. But the first time I took the drug at all, a snort one night in Paris, there was no sense of burnt bridges: the three of us were sitting in my hotel room, the bottles, as always, were close at hand and someone suggested getting high on something different. Just what was so special about heroin?

With Geoff as The Man, we crushed a couple of pills onto a sheet of paper, added a trace of cocaine ('It spices it up,' said Geoff), and sniffed it through a rolled up ten-franc note. We sat for a while to get the effect—Geoff cleaning his shoes slowly and compulsively, Gerry scratching his poker face—before going out to a club.

It was a heavy, physical high even in the tiny quantities we had taken. At first all I could taste was the intense and nauseating bitterness of the powder as I sat on the side of a bed, waiting. But gradually the sandpaper feeling in my throat turned into a numbness and that numbness became a warm glow, spreading down my spine and into the legs, up the neck to the back of my head, until my whole body felt charged and my brain tingled.

I stood up, swaying. In some subtle way the relationship between me and the outside was altered; my vision was clear but concentrated on the end of my nose. I was receiving sets of signals, slowly, both from the extremities of my body and from the surroundings and objects that I touched—but there didn't seem to be any distinction between the two.

Before leaving I stared in wonder at the rest of the tablets, so tiny, so harmless and neutral-looking, no bigger than a match head. I had been prepared for many reactions, anticipating something different from mere intoxication. What I had been totally unprepared for was this feeling of integration. And something more: a direct feeling of friendliness from the drug. I hadn't expected the chemical embrace.

When we went out it was as though events were being put on for me, as in a theatre. I was passive, totally receptive, nothing mattered; there were no distinctions. If someone had been shot dead in front of me in the Paris street I would have stood there, rocking gently, waiting incuriously to see what would be laid on me next. The evening passed in a haze of detachment and certainty.

Later on, once the cocaine had worn off and the heroin had reached its peak, a strong, sedative effect ensued. Then all the wires got crossed and one entered a strange, twilit world with half-closed eyes, unsure what was real and what wasn't—falling into a limbo of confusion between inner space and outer, half-remembered thoughts, odd snatches of sound, pieces of music, peoples' voices shooting across the screen of the mind.

After we'd left the club that night I felt like this—on the nod—and went for a stumbling walk by the Seine to try and clear my head. It was very late, cool and silent with hardly anyone on the streets, and after buying a crepe from the old lady's stall I found a spot to sit down at and stare at the water until I dropped off.

I awoke with a feeling of horrible emptiness and disorientation, not knowing where I was or what I'd been doing. Directly in front of me I thought I could see the figure of a woman, dressed in only a shift, apparently about to jump into the water. Visions of Ophelia. But it was only Pat. She turned round before I could speak.

'If he's sent you down here to talk me out of it you're wasting your time. And you can bloody well tell him so.'

I stood there, feeling very tired.

'No, Pat,' I said, 'I haven't come to talk you out of it.' And I wandered off to find a better riverbank before going to bed. Behind me I heard footsteps running; Gerry must be on his way to patch things up again.

But what strange worlds junk opened up! Hints of another galaxy inside the head: a new relationship of space and time. A day or two later I tried it again. And a few days later again. Just for a little while. . . .

Over the next week or two I spent more time with Geoff than I had done previously; perhaps taking smack together gave us more of a common language. But there was a change in him. In Sweden he'd had a burst of outwardness when he'd been pulling chicks all the time, talking more, involved with other people. Now he began to limit others again, keeping them away from his centre, his eyes even more fixed on his private horizons. Sometimes when we took stuff he seemed to open up more, but only for a short time. I knew that taking heroin must have accounted for some of the change, but it was only when he told me that he'd been sneaking pills out of the bottles ever since we'd left Scandinavia that I realized how far it went. It was like watching someone travelling away to an unknown land.

His visitor's passport was invalid for travel through Yugoslavia and he decided to leave us in Austria, taciturn and unforthcoming about where he intended to go. On the day we separated we were driving through the Alps, the four of us talking idly about what he might do—he knew a girl who was living in Salzburg and he thought he might go there—when Gerry went too fast in the snow and lost control of the car. We went into a long, fearsome weave downhill, scattering skiers in all directions, bouncing off the snowbanks one side and ripping out a section of fence on the other, bad, side before running the car into a huge pile of snow as the only way to stop.

With nothing to do except stare at the drop beneath us and listen to Pat's cries I began to get worried; when the back of the car went through the fence, rear wheels actually crumbling the edge, I gave it all up—and saw Geoff sitting there quite motionless, not even tensed and absolutely without expression. Not a muscle moved.

We dropped him near a station somewhere between Salzburg and the Wurzen. He told us he'd probably go and visit the girl and perhaps learn to ski. But as he stood outside the car I knew abruptly and for certain that he was going straight back to London: to a doctor to get registered for junk again. I said goodbye, I hoped he'd be lucky, maybe even careful; he gave us one of his grins and we left him in the snow.

There was a lot of time to think during the next few days because we could hardly get out of the car. We just got into Yugoslavia before the only pass closed again (gritting its top fifty metres ourselves with gear borrowed from a roadside shed) and the weather broke up completely. We had no chains or studded tyres and the Slavs had given up trying to keep the roads clear or usable: the drive south was a bad dream of sheet ice and snow, wrecked cars by the roadside, full hotels and the glare and hiss of emergency lights as the faltering rescue services tried to cope with yet another crash.

And my mind dwelled on Geoff and on the heaviness that taking junk could involve. But I didn't think of heroin as essentially either the villain or the enigma. The real mystery lay in the human being taking the drug, like Geoff, like myself. Geoff wasn't physically hooked, hadn't been fixing, had no provable need for heroin: it was seeing him moving away before he'd even got hooked that was chilling. Watching his will, his inner determination, to resort to a junk plane. If the will was already in pursuit of addiction how could it ever be used against the drug?

The sun came out just once in those few days and that was when we passed through Skopje, still sprawled out after the earthquake. I looked around at the scattered buildings, heaps of rubble, broken concrete tenements like spilled matches—inhabitants scratching for a living in tents, shacks, in the mud. This was turning into a destruction trip.

If I'd ever been thinking seriously about buying hashish I wasn't any longer once we reached Istanbul. The country was under martial law and there had been an assassination attempt; from the border to the capital little knots of armed troops stood at the road junctions and villages. And the new government had begun a purge of dope dealers and shot two of them to encourage the others. Then there'd been a gun battle between American undercover men and heroin traffickers resulting in a couple more deaths. Finally a consignment of tinned food had been opened up at the border (a bribe had gone wrong) and a load more junk and hashish discovered.

So there was a panic on. The result: hash was either unobtainable, except in tiny one-smoke deals, or costing a ridiculous price—$200 a kilo. The small-time villains who normally acted as connections between buyers and sellers turned temporarily to a safer trade: the US Sixth Fleet was in and they were busy mulcting the sailors.

Not wanting to buy and with my money beginning to run short anyway, I was able to look at all this with a certain amount of detachment. But Gerry was determined to score some at a cheaper price and wanted to go further into Turkey before going back. I felt like London again, for a while, and was in favour of going back there when I'd seen a bit more of the country. I could either get the train or wait for Gerry, and the heroin was with Gerry. . . .

After a few days we set off. It was a strikingly beautiful land to drive through but at that time of year dreadfully barren. As we drove further into the country without finding anyone who'd sell, I began to feel a sense of futility and also unreality. The gravel roads, the mud, sleet and flooding made the whole drive into hard work: the grimness of the succession of frozen and windy mountains, rainswept valleys, the harsh poverty of the land and the people began to depress me.

And there seemed to be an unpleasant and disturbing parallel between the journey and my own inner state. The split in my personality, the division between my willing pursuit of junk and my simultaneous forebodings that I was getting into something deeper than I'd ever expected, grew wider for a moment. All I could think was that I'd goofed, that I was halfway to Afghanistan in an alien land I didn't like; and halfway to outer space with a drug I didn't understand and wasn't fully master of. The future stretched away into the distance between the rocky peaks and rainsqualls, dark clouds, sheets of water cascading down the slopes.

We turned back. As a last resort when we reached Istanbul Gerry went to buy at the local price, deciding to work on a lower profit margin. But he was careless, trusted an intermediary too much and got heavily stoned on some local smoke before meeting the man with the gear. This wasn't Sweden though: the connection made a run for it with his bread and got away. I was torn between a detached annoyance at the cheek of the guy and a cynical admiration for anyone able to turn Gerry over.

'There's a curse on this fucking journey,' said Gerry as we headed for the Bulgarian frontier, scraping the Turkish mud off our shoes. I'd just taken another snort. It seemed funny, in a mad sort of way.

Finally we got to the frontier, after one more bad moment. (We were overcharged at a village garage. Gerry wouldn't pay and a bad row developed with the brothers who owned the garage. Violence ensued, I attacked one of them and it turned into a riot. They smashed in the back of the car as we fled.)

I was sleeping in the back of the car for a while and didn't wake up until about midnight when we were passing through Sophia. I stretched out, yawned and looked at the deserted, badly lit streets. A slight, dusting snow blew over the pavements.

As we headed down one of the central boulevards at about fifty miles an hour I stared idly at the only other vehicle on the road—a two-car tram coming towards us. Ahead of us, on our right, was a T-junction: without any warning the tram pulled directly across us towards the side road. I doubt if the driver saw us even, in any case there was very little Gerry could do. I braced myself against the seats as we tried to get round him and went into a long broadside, my last clear view being of the driver reaching for his warning bell and beginning to toll it as we hit him. . . .

There was never a chance of stopping in time. We hit the front end at forty-five degrees and the car simply caved in, broke up with an enormous bang and was dragged along, disintegrating, like a cow on a cow-catcher. In slow motion I watched the gearbox leave the floor, the front end spray open, the roof crush down, onto my head.

I woke up after perhaps a minute and kicked open the remainder of a back door, staggered out and sat down in the middle of the road. I was covered in blood. And all I could hear, over and over, were Pat's long, terrible screams echoing down the boulevard. I got up, fell over, got up again and stumbled over to the car where a confused claque of Bulgarians milled around, shouting and whistling. They were already helping Gerry out but Pat was trapped, smashed and unrecognizable. I turned away in a sort of numb despair, spitting out blood and putting my hands over my ears.

I was staring at the ceiling in a casualty department, brightly lit and cheerful. Doctors and nurses busied themselves professionally; Gerry lay on the next-door couch. For the first time I was conscious enough to start assessing the situation and I checked myself over, finding to my amazement that I wasn't badly hurt at all. Nothing was broken. I'd bitten through my tongue and lost a couple of teeth but apart from that—nothing. The blood on my clothes had come from a number of small cuts and, I suspect, from Pat.

I asked about her. They'd got her out of the wreck and were starting to operate, and there was a good chance she would live. Beside me Gerry was conscious, staggering around giving urine samples of a deeper and deeper hue. They were admitting him for internal damage and me for the state of my head. I lay back and let my mind drift, trying to remember just what had happened until something nagged at my memory — the gear in the car.

I sat up quickly. All the stuff had been under the dashboard when we hit and that meant it could be anywhere. I asked the doctor what was being done with the car. The police had impounded it. 'Well,' I said, 'it's urgent that one of us gets out to it, we've got valuables in there.' He gave me a doctor's calming look and said everything would be all right with the police; they would check and label all the belongings for us.

I lay back to gather my strength. Sick as he was Gerry had the horrors, too, and after he came over we turned our combined personalities onto the staff, inventing reasons as they came into our heads, insisting they get us a car to take us to the wreck. In the end they gave up and after dire warnings, especially to Gerry, they decided to humour us. We were wrapped in blankets and transported to the main entrance where a car was waiting for us with staff to get the stuff from the crash.

But it was a police car and the 'staff' were two fuzz. I told them I thought I was strong enough to sort it out myself without their help. The hospital was near the scene and we made it there in about five minutes, pulling into the road where a knot of locals stood staring at the bits of car strewn over an enormous radius. Two policemen stood by the remains, guarding them. I saw that they hadn't taken anything out; we were cool.

Grovelling in the wreckage amongst the broken glass, bits of metal and sticky blood, I found the preludin immediately—the tubes were all over the floor. The junk was harder to find, but as it had been wrapped in rags and cotton wool at least the bottles were unbroken. Gerry distracted the police for half a minute with his groans—they were real—and I scooped everything up into a briefcase. We drove back, shivering but at liberty. And that was enough for me. I was falling asleep again and I stayed asleep, except for brief intervals, for the next few days.

I was given a private room and a head specialist and stayed for ten days, being treated competently and by pleasant staff. The Piragoff was a brand-new hospital and they knew what they were doing. I saw Pat after a few days when they let me walk around; she was all right and full of praise for the things they had done for her. They had saved her legs although she was going to be damaged for the rest of her life: she was philosophical, a tough lady.

After a week of blood transfusions and some days on the critical list Gerry was allowed to get up for a few hours. He appeared at the door of my room, having fled his emergency ward without permission—they were dying off like flies in there and he was getting depressed. I got rid of the nurse and without another word Gerry went over to my locker, where the bottles were kept, and made up a couple of snorts. I took one with him but stared at him in surprise. I'd never seen him look so positive about stuff before.

Now he had time on his hands and the future didn't count; for the first time he sat around, stretched out and began really getting into the drug with determination. He'd always been too hustling, too speedy, too concerned with running—towards and away— to let himself drift with heroin. Now it was different. I didn't get the same sense with him over the next few days, as I had done with Geoff, of movement away to another level. Gerry switched planes all right, or began to, but with him it was a matter of sitting still and finding another area within himself, one that he'd never known existed. He stopped running for a moment —and found that he didn't know if he wanted to start running again, that he could relax.

Bulgaria was a funny country to be stuck in. It was both Balkan and very communist, and the combination led to scenes that we could never really master. As soon as we left the hospital there was a problem: to register at the hotel we had to leave our passports. But we'd only had forty-eight hour transit visas, now expired; manifestly the hotel couldn't accept the passports. So we couldn't stay there either. But what about renewing the visas? Well, that was very difficult; one could renew a visa that was due to expire, yes—but these had already expired, therefore they could not be renewed. Otherwise, said the passport people, you could come here with ten-year-old visas and renew them.

Most of our dealings with the authorities went like this. Bulgaria being a good communist country even the laying on of gold didn't help; the gold was laid and lost, without result. For the moment we bypassed the issue by pleading sickness, getting the Ministry of Health to ring the passport office and, finally using their own logic, stating that we were here, had not been arrested and therefore must have a right to be here. For the time being we got our hotel.

Now all I had to do was get out of the country, but that was even more difficult. I had no money left, not even enough to get home with, and not much prospect of getting any. I should have gone to the Consulate right away but I'd started making a scene with one of the hospital nurses and she had a brother, a high party official, who travelled to Western Europe a lot. Maria wanted to come too, and the result was I got hung up waiting to see if she could get an exit visa; if she had done we'd have had a ride to Paris without problems.

But things moved very slowly and I found myself waiting, piling up the hotel bills and spending some of Maria's money. A lot of time was spent at first in labyrinthine forays into the ministries of health and transport, trying to find out who paid the hospital bills and what sort of insurance money there might be.

But that was a dead loss. They seemed to make up the rules as they went along, and I began to lose interest. Whatever money might eventually transpire would be in Bulgarian, mickey mouse currency, non-negotiable and useless outside the country. It's hard to describe the difficulties involved in trying to deal with a semi-Stalinist —and incompetent—bureaucracy when there are no precedents. The one result (apart from the imprisonment of the tram-driver, which we'd hardly wanted) was that they waived the hospital bills. That's more than would have happened in the States, I guess.

After a while we began to tire. Gerry was still a sick man and under treatment, and he began to look bad again; it was all too much. Rather than begin fighting with the immigration people again or dodge the militia-men who followed us around, we'd stay in the hotel burning down the H and C, getting more and more stoned and hallucinatory. Soon we were keeping the doors locked so that the staff couldn't see the state we were reducing their rooms to: empty pill and wine bottles, preludin phials, odd women's clothing, rolled up mickey mouse money all round the floor. And I took to charging everything to room service, calling to them to leave the tray in the hall outside the door.

It couldn't last. After two weeks, pale, wan and staggering I found I couldn't get my lift and Maria couldn't get her visa. The hotel bill was now colossal, unpaid since the beginning, and the management started to get unpleasant. The passport office took to giving us one-day extensions, calling in the militia to throw us out when we objected. The British Consul, a withdrawn and lonely creature behind his legation's steel shutters, observed our scenes with distaste and mounting concern. I copped out and asked him to get me back to England.

There was a little difficulty over the hotel bills— to put it mildly—but by now the Consulate were getting the horrors that we might cause an 'incident' and they dug up an emergency fund for helping car crash victims. They would fly Pat home when she was well enough to move. Gerry was staying on for a few more days for further out-patient treatment and a last attempt at compensation. In any case he'd set the wheels moving and they wouldn't stop; he was now enmeshed and would have to return later in the year to go through the Bulgarian courts. For the moment he wasn't so broke, having received eighty dollars and a three-page contract for the car. They bought it for scrap, 'without prejudice'.

On my last day there the two of us went to visit Pat. I felt relieved to be going at last and for the first time in weeks I was able to enjoy the beauty of the capital. Spring was on its way and the cherry trees were beginning to blossom, although it was very gusty that day and a few drops of rain began to fall as we got off the tram outside the hospital.

The Piragoff, as I said, was new and Sophia's pride and joy: 'the most up-to-date hospital in the Balkans'. As we walked to the entrance a sudden, hard squall blew up, raising the dust and papers in the street. I heard a strange shrieking noise and looking up saw that the entire roof, flat riveted zinc sheeting, had started to lift off. I went on staring as it floated upwards, flapping and undulating twelve stories up and clear of the walls before going into a curving downward glide. It was some moments before I realized just how much metal there was in that roof and by then I was running for cover. It came down onto the tram wires with a brilliant cracking blue flash and broke up into half a dozen huge chunks of metal, one or two of which rolled down the street like space capsules, Bulgars jumping into doorways along their route.

Gerry stood beside me looking at the shambles and munching an apple.

'Everything breaks up in this bloody country,' he said morosely, 'everything put together falls apart.' It sounded like a requiem. We went to see if it was raining in on Pat.

I said I'd see them both in London. Gerry was going to head for Stockholm first to try and sell the preludin and heroin. But there wasn't much heroin left any more and by the time he got to Sweden I doubted if there'd be any.

I knew where I was going. That split had closed up now and the forebodings were gone, or far at the back of my mind. In any case it was too late to turn back now. As soon as I got off the train at Victoria I was getting a cab to the West End to score some more heroin and a disposable syringe to fix it with.

3

I'd only been in Piccadilly twenty minutes or so when I saw Geoff standing by one of the underground exits. I was already moving across the road towards him when he looked up and saw me; he was smiling but thin and haggard-looking. We both started talking at once and moved off to get a cup of coffee in the sandwich bar across the Circus. I didn't feel like talking much about the business in Bulgaria and he seemed to be slightly stoned and not taking things in too well.

He told me how he'd been repatriated from somewhere in Italy and had started using regularly when he got back. I waited for a chance to interrupt.

'Have you got anything on you now?' I asked. He started grinning again.

'You've got that look, Tony; I thought you'd get into stuff.' He paused, perhaps for effect, while I listened to the traffic on the Circus. 'I could get hold of some shortly.'

'Well, come back to my place and fix it then. I'd be a bit worried on my own.' Which was true. I got the horrors at the thought of embolisms and accidents like that. Maybe I needed moral support. Geoff finished his coffee and asked me for a pound to score with. I arranged to meet him in half an hour in the Underground.

And I finished my drink on my own, glancing at a newspaper, anticipating. After half an hour I split to the tube and found Geoff nodding off on a platform bench. He slept until we got to Clapham; I read the posters over and over.

In the pad he pulled out a paper bag containing disposable plastic syringes. I noticed that the needles were unpleasantly long and thick. I also noticed a subtle, if transient, change in our relationship: Geoff was the man who knew what things were about. I was just a pupil.

'These were the only needles I could get,' he said, following my stricken gaze. 'Have you got a spoon? And a glass of water?' I moved about for him and he split one of the tiny heroin tablets in half with his thumbnail, laying it in the spoon. He half-filled the teaspoon with water, struck a match and began to cook the mixture up. I watched, fascinated and agitated, as the pill began to bubble and dissolve. A strong, hardly definable smell filled the room, medicinal and smoky. I began to feel dizzy.

'That smell gets to you when you've used before,' said Geoff dreamily, blowing out the match. 'Some people throw up as soon as they sniff the fumes.' Carefully he dipped the end of the needle into the spoon and drew the liquid up into the works. 'All for you.'

I took the syringe and pushed the plunger up until most of the air was expelled, as I'd seen nurses doing. My hands shook.

'Don't mess about with veins first time,' Geoff said. 'Just stick it in the muscle, and don't worry about a bit of air.'

I rolled up my sleeve. The needle was enormous. When I pressed it against the skin nothing happened. I couldn't make myself prod hard enough. Geoff watched me, saw me sweating and asked if I wanted him to do it. I didn't. This was for no-one but me. I watched the skin on my arm concave around the needle point and thought for a moment: there was no going back from a fix, wherever it led. Perhaps some of the comments I'd heard about junkies in the past came back to me. In any case I held on, hesitating, with a sort of roaring in my ears until I ended the debate with a sharp, vicious jab into the skin of my forearm. Slowly I pressed the plunger and watched the gear forming a little lump under the skin. Slowly still I pulled the works out and stared into space; the roaring in my ears was gone.

For pernaps two minutes I sat there, unspeaking, before the stuff hit me properly. It was like a punch in the stomach, a soft gripping of the insides, followed by an intense tingling in the limbs. The feeling began to envelop me, a passive orgasm all over my body, almost taking my breath away. Forbidden fruit. Then the buzz reached my mind and I stopped thinking about significance, staggered over to the bed and lay back feeling out of it, right out of it, scratching my stomach lazily. None of it mattered.

Geoff knocked up a fix for himself while I lay there and

talked dreamily, my voice coming from deep at the back of my throat, the words stretching out, running into one another. I asked him if he was registered with a doctor for stuff. He said no, the doctor he'd been to before wouldn't take him on yet. He was hustling money from girls in the West End and scoring regularly from one junky he knew well.

'But I'm running out of girls so I might see him again soon. I don't know.' He had the old hopelessness back in his eyes more strongly than ever.

'Do you really want to get registered?' I asked, in my beginner's way.

'No choice,' he replied, 'you'll see for yourself sometime.'

'Why do you want to go on using?'

'Because there's nothing else like it. I prefer it even to chicks.'

We talked on for a while and then I felt the smack beginning to overtake me and drifted off into a warm sleep.

Six hours later I woke up with a jump: it was dark outside and getting cold. Geoff was sprawled out in an armchair, the skin stretched tight over his face. I started shivering and went out to get something to eat, leaving Geoff and his deathmask behind. I felt fear at the back of my mind again, but a fear that I couldn't name.

Over the next few days I used the rest of the heroin that Geoff had scored, a half pill at a time. The effect lasted most of the day and after shooting up I'd sit around reading, listening to music and feeling the buzz. After a week I got some more off Geoff and then he vanished, presumably arrested; so I left it alone for a while, not feeling too happy about scoring off strangers. I knew I'd be into it again soon enough.

A week later Gerry appeared at my door again in front of a filthy, travel-stained Renault. He was broke and his head had been moving in the same direction as mine: he wanted a turn-on. That was almost the first thing he told me. We wiped some of the mud off the car and drove around the West End, minicabbing, until we'd raised some money. Scoring was such a hustle. Neither of us knew any of the junkies in Piccadilly and we couldn't locate any likely-looking strangers to ask. We went from the Circus to a pub in Charlotte Street, from there to another pub, got the name of a user from one of the boys in the bar and finally, four hours after we began, drove to an address in West Kensington and picked up off a wasted little Canadian boy called Mike.

Some people get a kick from the aggravation connected with scoring; it makes it more adventurous, there's more of a build-up. But during all the waiting around I was thinking of the chances of getting stuff legally from a doctor, anything to avoid this business every time I wanted gear—and I knew I wanted gear fast and often. I was thinking about it some more while Gerry made himself a fix back at my place and banged it into his arm quick as smiling, squirting the remnants from the works into his mouth.

Gerry wasn't too well, very thin and slightly yellow-looking. His kidneys, he told me, hadn't recovered properly and nobody knew when they would. Pat had dropped out of the picture and gone back to her parents. And all his preludin had been taken off him at the Yugoslav border, leaving him only the junk to sell. In Stockholm he'd bought the car for twenty pounds worth of stuff and had driven back here as quickly as he could. Stockholm was madder than ever and when he was snorting smack he couldn't take the pace; there was too much speed and paranoia.

'But it's such a drag having to score again in London,' he said.

'Well,' I replied, 'I was just thinking about that.'

Gerry stayed for the next few days; we spent the time shooting up and searching for doctors. No-one seemed very keen to help us. The Canadian kid finally gave us two names, one in the East End of London who was supposed to be easy to get on with, and another in Chelsea who was unpredictable. The next time the stuff ran short we drove over to the East End.

The surgery was next to a railway viaduct in the hard part of dockland. The waiting room spooked me out; there were about half a dozen people in there, all in a shocking state, looking ill but somehow different from ordinary patients: some of them had their arms swathed in bandages and one, a bespectacled old woman, was on crutches. I felt an oppressive air of menace in the room. Were these junkies? I didn't know. I didn't stay to find out. I wasn't going through all that every time I wanted a script. The next day I stuck a few more pinholes in my arm to make it look as if I'd been using longer and went to see Dr Robert in Chelsea.

This was better: the waiting room had plenty of normal people in it—nothing like the sinister East End scene. I gave a name—false—to the receptionist and after ten minutes went in to see the quack. He was a friendly-looking man about forty years of age, going bald on top. He sat at his desk and gave me a grin.

'What can I do for you?'

I found it hard to say. 'It's about drugs,' I murmured, diffidently, 'I've become addicted to heroin.'

I expected some sort of heavy reaction but he didn't express any surprise, started taking some details and asking me questions. How long and how much?

'About a year. Three grains a day.' The lies slipped easily off my tongue. If I told him the truth I wasn't going to get anything. He asked me to roll up my sleeves, looked briefly and sat down to write a prescription. I was registered. He asked me to come back in a week and I left with the scripts in my hand, holding the door open for Gerry on my way out.

It felt funny picking up the prescription. I watched the pharmacist measuring out the pills, half-expecting a policeman to come in and start questioning me. It was upside-down, I was getting a supply of drugs that were one hundred per cent illegal in my experience and here was a chemist doling them out under bright lights with a doctor's O.K. I was a legal citizen.

The idea was to give you drugs to support a habit once it had become incurable. It was always difficult for doctors to work out the long-term addicts from the beginners, although the system worked well as long as not many people used junk. And characters like me didn't help—there was a certain lack of frankness in my story. Later on there was a panic at easy availability and prescribing was restricted.

But that was a long time away. In 1964 junk wasn't a 'problem' and we were left alone. I picked up a three-day prescription for nine grains of heroin, fifty-four pills, and went off to have a fix in a hotel lavatory, secure in the knowledge I wouldn't be busted.

PART TWO

THE CITY

4

It's relatively uncommon for someone to get registered as quickly as I did. A few people go on sniffing smack for years without ever injecting it. Others start fixing but avoid getting hold of large quantities for as long as possible, partly because a regular supply brings them face-to-face with the possibility of addiction for the first time. But I knew what I wanted and didn't worry very much about total dependence; although whether my idea of dependence tallied with the reality was another matter.

Having found my path, I let junk very quickly become an integral part of life, more important to me—voluntarily at that time—than anything else. I adjusted very easily, building my activities around junk rather than adding it to them. I solved my money problems by getting hold of some weights of hashish and selling it to people I knew. Selling hash wasn't arduous and I still liked the potheads I dealt with.

I didn't want to stay in Battersea for long. There were some straight people who knew me and who asked questions that I couldn't answer; it was useless trying to explain where I was at, and after a while useless even to talk. Straight people usually just got frightened at the hint or mention of junk.

The landlady got weird as well. She had worked out that something was going on—not too difficult given the circumstances of junk life—and her erstwhile motherly attitude towards me turned into fear and revulsion. She communicated only at night and only if there was too much noise, never showing herself. Two or three of us would be sitting in the flat and we'd hear a fast scratching—scratching, not knocking—on the door. By the time I got there she was gone and there would be a note, pushed underneath or left outside. 'You are making too much noise. Just what are you doing in there?' She gave us the shivers.

It was slightly disturbing to see how people's reactions to me could change when they found out that I was involved with stuff: understandable but still disturbing. Still, I stayed on for a while longer and a girl I knew locally moved in with me. Apart from her I found myself seeing mostly those connected, one way or another, with drugs.

Annette accepted the fact of junk, as women often did, perhaps thinking it was a temporary aberration, perhaps for other reasons. She was a dancer, not long out of ballet school where she had been the star student. A small and beautiful girl of astonishing grace, she had recently broken up with her boyfriend and turned to me as someone familiar. She didn't use stuff.

We stayed together intermittently over several months. During that time we rarely made it together. Junk took away much of my sexual desire at first and it began to alter my whole emotional approach to others. They became just less desirable, fine to meet but not really worth pursuing; the emotional tension went out of my relations with them. I never knew how much I cared for Annette; perhaps I was indifferent—junk can be like that.

One got into other changing patterns. I couldn't eat a meal for a month without being sick; food became a tiresome necessity, a fuel to keep me going; taste wasn't important. Money lost its value except to buy immediate or impulse things: syringes, coca cola, taxis to the chemist's—there wasn't much I wanted that I didn't have. I started to get turned on to junk time, another scale of measurement, independent of clocks, night or day, a time operating from within and geared firstly to junk itself, and then to its ancillaries: doctors, chemists, other junkies, what the body signalled.

I began to spend a lot of time in the dope areas around London, particularly in Ladbroke Grove. When Annette was away touring with her ballet company I stayed with a rich Irish whore named Gloria who owned a flat in Powis Terrace.

That was a mad street. There was a whole Rachman programme going on whereby the street, which had housed ordinary working people, was being turned over. Rachman had encouraged whores and the more dubious Jamaicans to move into his houses; they brought the neighbours down until they couldn't stand it any more and split. Sometime later the flats would be sold as expensive dwellings for the middle classes. While I was there the process was still going on and it was social chaos, the kind of looseness that attracted people like myself. The street was dead in the morning, woke up late afternoon and moved all night, in a haze of dope.

You could wander along to the Escarpelette coffee house where Steve kept his electric organ ready to play in one corner and the loo was filled with San Francisco graffiti; or to the head shop next door (West Coast poets, Charlie Mingus records, pamphlets and posters); or to a shebeen, a basement drinking house for Jamaicans with a slot in the door to suss you out and loud blue beat music and stocks of ganja, West Indian grass blown long and thick in the halflight.

So much grass! It was like a vegetable market. And freaks like Nicky Douglas, who had a collection of hash which he never smoked but produced from a carrier bag, would lecture on the way different hash illustrated different cultures. A lot of philistines tried to steal that bag.

Underneath the head shop Michael de Freitas—Michael X—held court, but that was before he was into love and peace and other ventures: he ran a sharp poker game and had a flash scene going, wearing pinstripe suits, white cuffs and short hair. And there were a lot of musicians living in the street; so you could always start at one flat and move on later to others, each time hearing different groups of people playing, each time getting loaded on smack, joints, coke-sniffing. A dope culture.

Most of the crowd I began to hang around with at this time were using drugs the same way as I was—I didn't know many long-time junkies well. Some of them were musicians, some writers or artists, others were just hipsters, people into getting high and hustling. And there were others who were hard to make out, like a couple of young burglars who used, one or two stylish kite artists (people who specialized in false cheques), and some drop-outs from good families. Junk tied together people from a whole variety of backgrounds.

There was Max, who'd been a burglar himself once but who now, after years of bizarre hustling, was an executive with a record company at a vast salary. Max was from the

North Country and called people 'mun': yes mun, no mun. He was a small, thin, wiry guy with receding hair who never had the blood pressure to make his veins stand up; whenever he fixed he swung his arm round and round for ten minutes before hitting. We called him the phantom windmill and cleared half the room for him. Max had gear under a sporadic control and every now and then he'd vanish to the States or Europe on business, purposely taking no stuff with him. He'd return even more shrunken and wiry, but without a habit.

When he did get a hit he made it to the bathroom to be sick and returned talking faster and faster, occasionally glancing at the works still stuck in his arm. He talked of conspiracies, which he saw all around him and some of which he'd been involved in—of business deals and ventures of ridiculous complexity, of the soul, of poetry and black magic and of Billy Graham whom he hated.

Spike and Clare were already registered. Drop-out Spike had been brought back from the alleys of Tangier by Max to join the company and had married Clare, the heiress, whose family were trying to stop her getting her millions as long as she went on using. She was a fragile beauty, a blonde model whose looks were already being attacked by junk and who played it closer to the line than any of us, not getting really turned on unless she'd pumped in enough for a borderline overdose. Then we wrapped wet flannels round her head while she sat swaying, refusing to remove the works in case she missed something.

I met Phil Seamen at Gloria's. He was an old-time junky and something of a legend for his junk capacity as well as his music. First time we met he sat quietly, nodding off and untalkative, his shockingly haggard face drooping into the corner of his chair. A couple of weeks later I was walking along Kensington High Street when I saw someone lying on his stomach on the pavement, his face pressed up against a shop window. It was Phil.

'Hello, man,' I said and stopped. 'Are you all right?'

He looked up and said hello casually, ignoring a couple of curious onlookers. 'Sure I'm all right.'

'What are you doing?' I asked, starting to laugh.

'It's a shoe shop, Tony. I'm buying a pair of shoes.'

'Why are you down there?'

'I'm looking at the soles of the shoes,' he explained patiently. 'You ever buy shoes without looking at the soles?'

I went to a gig of his that night. Of course he hadn't shown on time and the other musicians started to play as best they could without a drummer. There was a stumbling noise half-way through the first number. Phil lurched in, cigarette in mouth, swayed over to the drums and picked up the sticks, starting to play with one hand, removing his raincoat with the other. Once he got down to it, all the fumbling vanished: he played like lightning.

I did my first junk deal around this time, a couple of months after getting registered. I was at Max's place in the Fulham Road and he was going to Tangier the next morning for a few weeks; this time he wanted to take gear with him. I had plenty of stuff still and agreed to sell. Max the fast hustler took over. The normal price was a pound a grain; if he took a lot off me I should surely agree to sell it more cheaply—like wholesale terms. That was the way he put it. I finally sold him thirty grains—everything I had surplus—and he thanked me profusely. That would just last him until he returned.

I spent a lot of time at Spike's flat in South Kensington, Powis Terrace rather tiring me out. One night we were wondering when Max was coming back.

'Well,' I said, 'he's got plenty of stuff with him, he won't have to hurry.'

'No he hasn't,' Spike answered, 'he was round the night before he left and he sold us all the stuff he had to help us out.'

'Just how much was that?' I asked, quietly.

'Twenty grains. At a pound a grain, the sod. Said he'd had to pay twenty-five shillings.'

But I always forgave Max, that was just his way. And besides I soon found out that it was like a merry-go-round: someone was always selling stuff and then buying back a few days later, usually at the same price. Once I was using myself I felt no qualms about selling junk.

One morning I woke up at Spike's without any gear and there was none in the flat to buy or borrow; I had to get a new prescription from Doctor Robert. For the first time I felt rough. Walking along Gloucester Road to the surgery I felt my legs getting weak as though they were about to give way.

I thought maybe I was ill, but by the time I reached the doctor's I was sweating and shaky and realized that I had a trace of withdrawal.

Doctor Robert gave me a quick script ('suffering a bit this morning?') and I grabbed a cab to the nearest junk chemist. There I sat and shivered while the pharmacist made up the prescription. I collected the stuff, bought a disposable works and made a run for the lavatory in a nearby cinema. The weakness eased away as soon as I turned on.

I shouldn't have been surprised; I'd been using daily for two or three months and had built up a modest habit of about a grain a day. But I hadn't thought of myself as near to real addiction. I had already decided that if junk appeared to be getting a serious hold on me then I would come off for a while—to show that I could control it. But sitting in the lavatory as the fix worked its way through, I didn't see the situation as serious enough for immediate action; I would give it some more time. Besides, I hadn't been really sick, just uncomfortable; it hardly counted really . . . the empty syringe swung in my hand.

What size was a real habit? Most people I knew thought a grain was the minimum you could be hung up on; but no-one was sure because you never stayed on a grain for long, it seemed like a threshold or take-off point. An 'average' habit at that time was three to four grains, anything bigger was getting out of hand.

Those who knew him thought Phil Seamen was the biggest user of all, followed closely by Bill Burroughs. There were others who used almost as much but who didn't come into the reckoning—the write-off junkies, the ones who were always on the floor or in hospital ('no fookin' style,' said Max). If you did count them, then there was Moss who used twenty grains of smack and twenty of cocaine every day and it still wasn't enough. But Moss was totally taken over, possessed by junk, covered in scars from the chemist's windows he'd broken through, one eye missing, sleeping rough and filthy dirty.

Cocaine made things worse unless you stuck to sniffing it. There was no withdrawal from coke, but once you started digging it you tended to blow a whole script at one sitting.

Coke on its own was useless, though; so you made cocktails (called speedballs, whizzbangs) with smack—and of course your heroin consumption and level of addiction went up.

I had a small script for coke but I never liked it as much as my friends did; I seemed to be over-sensitive to it and was always risking an overdose. One night I made a bad blunder with the amount in the works and shot in three or four times as much as I'd ever fixed before, with less smack to counteract it.

As soon as I'd put it in I knew something was wrong. Coke gives you a strong, fresh rush to the head like a breeze in your brain and it comes upwards at you from your chest to your neck until your head fills; then the body buzz of the heroin takes over and the two balance out. This time it was all chaos and I felt the coke charge up my neck like a swollen piston before it hit my head and the syringe jumped out of my arm, my arching back jerking me to my feet.

All I could do was stagger over to the open window to try and breathe while Annette poured bowl after bowl of cold water over me. I felt as if I was going to ignite. In five minutes the panic was over; if you were still conscious then you were all right. I sat shakily in a chair and decided to be a bit careful with charlie in future.

Smack had its nightmares as well but in a different form: a one-shot overdose wasn't so common. There was a gradual build-up over a period of hours until the organism began to rebel; then you started hallucinating and getting the horrors, stuck in a twilight consciousness. I'd go for a walk in the fresh air, frightened and cold, a bizarre sight to passers-by as I ducked and weaved between imaginary obstacles, pursued by ghosts.

But the nightmares and obsessions were never enough to put me off; perhaps they fascinated me at a deeper level than the more obvious pleasures of junk. In any case I carried on using, my intake rising weekly: seven pills, grain-and-a-half, two grains a day within four months of getting registered.

And I carried on with the frivolous, early-junky routine. Up in the morning and out to the chemist or doctor. Hang around the West End for a while, looking in the shops, buying clothes. Bump into a friend, back to his place to fix, sit about getting stoned, maybe sell him some hash. Nodding off in restaurants over a coffee and pastry, reading the same magazine over and over, the words floating on the page. Catch some music in the evening, back to a flat—Spike's, where I was now living most of the time, or a variety of others—sitting round in groups again shooting up all night long, drinking coffee, smoking dope, playing music, talking, sniffing coke, getting higher, higher. People dropping off, a guy painting in the corner of the room, walk the streets at dawn to freshen up, phone for food to be sent in, shoot some coke to wake up, the pad gradually disintegrating, empty cups, dirty plates, syringes, tissues strewn about the flat. A few hours' sleep, a bath, the whole cycle starting again, three, four day bursts like this, drawn curtains, smoke in the room.

The all-night conversations, the chance meetings soared off into another, unrecognizable world. The circumstances that surrounded junk took one into a strange, phantasmagoric existence where the outrageous became routine, where sudden excitement and random disaster were equally close, where bizarre rumours could never be disproved, where nothing could be believed.

The junk world was a mad underside of the normal surface with leads and threads that disappeared into the shadows: a Middle Eastern potentate was on the phone from his hotel, trying to score; John was an ex-CIA man hustling opium, strangely knowledgeable about Kennedy's death; Phil had been found dead from an overdose that morning—was it true? This copper used stuff himself, would take a bribe; this minister's son was a junkie, blackmail was being paid, you'd probably meet him tomorrow; Archie had just been shot dead in Nepal.

And the weeks and months passed with me feeling so cool, looking down on it all, feeling that I could never be captured by the manifest evil that junk enclosed, wondering when I would feel like coming off.

Spike had invited Annette and me to share the big flat in Gloucester Road permanently, partly because we genuinely liked each other, partly because I still had some surplus stuff on my script. I'd only been using Battersea for dealing hash for a couple of months; I went back there one evening to pick up a couple of ounces and some of my belongings. The fuzz were waiting on the doorstep.

A friendly chat. The old style, a fat copper and a thin one; one noisy, one silent. I had no opportunity to hide the hash and it lay on the table in a plastic bag while we talked, with me getting more and more nervous as I waited to see if they would start searching the place.

They asked me about Sweden and what I'd been doing there. How much junk was I using now? More questions and then the atmosphere began to ease up; I was suddenly aware of a vibe in the room—they felt sorry for me, genuinely pitied me. Was I that sick a figure now? I couldn't make it out, but I went along with it just in case, playing things the way they wanted to.

They had some coffee, watched me nervously clearing the table (and stashing the weed away) and got up to leave.

'By the way,' said the fat one, 'I came to arrest you tonight. False name, false address to the doctor. Fraud.'

I started to mutter excuses, something about my family, fear of publicity—

'Just get it changed tomorrow,' cut in the officer; 'now I'm going before I change my mind.' I remembered that inspector.

Everyone was scared of being busted. Not for the sentence but for the horror scene in Brixton when you couldn't get a pill. A medical remand in prison was almost inevitable for a junky once he'd turned up at the court, however light the charge, however small the eventual penalty. Even with my relatively light habit I'd heard too many stories of what went on, seen too many addicts come out in small pieces. You couldn't learn to cope with a prison cold turkey—some people didn't try and knocked themselves off the night before court or, occasionally, in Brixton itself.

I told Dr Robert about the scripts and gave him my real name. He was nice about it; so I hit him for an increase of half a grain while he was feeling charitable. Keep a safety margin. But I'd found that being registered for junk was something different from the normal patient-doctor relationship. Doctor Robert was likely to get moody and feel he was being exploited; if you caught him on a trip like that then you had to keep talking and lay things on in order to avoid having your script cut.

Like most of the junk doctors, private or GP, he was ambivalent towards addicts, wanting to help and also needing them, aware of the personal power his role gave him and sometimes guilty about it. And he was gay, which made things worse. You didn't have to worry about pressure to sleep with him; you worried when he started to care for you, in his own mixed-up way, for then he gave you a hard time, full of conflicts about whether he was helping or killing you by giving you stuff. You tried to stay invisible and not give him anything to care about.

Scripts were cashed either at a local chemist who stocked gear because he was near a doctor or, if one needed stuff badly, at one of the all-night chemists in town. There were two—Boots, Piccadilly, and John Bell and Croydon, in Wigmore Street. Boots was a bring-down drag. It had all the hardest cases going there, the homeless ones, the filthy ones, staggering around loaded on sleeping pills to hold the sickness at bay until they picked up the next day's scripts on the stroke of midnight. Not surprisingly the staff didn't like junkies.

Bell's was cooler and most of the time it was gentleman junkies and quiet Americans from Lady Frankau's surgery down the road. They had a pleasant waiting room where you could sit while your script was done, a big circular tropical-fish tank in the centre of the room to soothe troubled nerves. I'd drop a jack of heroin into the tank to turn the fishes on. After a while I found out half-a-dozen other addicts were doing the same thing, no doubt creating a mutant race of fish junkies. On the whole they looked more *together* than the human ones.

I ran into Moss at Boots one midnight. We went for a turn-on together and he insisted on laying a fix on me. After a cup of coffee and a bit of rapping, he launched into a long scene about picking his next script up in North London and needing gear until he got over there. Somehow I found myself parting with a couple of grains until the next morning. Moss tended to do that to people he didn't know: I didn't see him for a week and then he pretended he'd never met me.

Moss was funny that way. Years later, not long before he killed himself, he told me how he searched out 'fresh'-looking junkies to con: 'just to hit that innocence, so they'd begin to know how hard it was.' Did I look that fresh then? I asked. 'Well,' he said, 'you didn't look like you'd done two years before the mast, Tony. You were cocky-looking. But then you're still cocky-looking.'

Junky chat and the junky con were something else. However much you were on your guard the sheer, pressing need to get more stuff enabled a strung-out addict to wind himself up, to raise himself to a near-manic state of persuasion until you felt yourself giving way even though the gear you lent wasn't going to come back. That need always gave a sick junky an edge, you were always going to tire before he did.

As my face became known, so I would be approached by other users in the street or outside chemists and I could often be an easy touch—especially as I expected to need stuff myself from other people now and then. But it was difficult not to get hardened after a while, not to build up a callousness to other people's needs, a partial indifference to suffering. One could hardly help everybody. Most of my own circle of junky friends could take care of themselves better than I could: it was the casual outside circle of users that I came into contact with, the knock-down users, the street addicts, who worried me more.

At first I thought the street addicts were just junkies at a later stage with their addiction finally out of control. But it wasn't quite like that; there were junkies on the streets who'd once been much more together but there were also many who hadn't in fact been using for very long, some of them cracking up after only a few months of being registered. And the process could be observed day by day. A young guy would be seen around the West End with plenty of surplus on his script, registered a few days. As you met him over the next couple of months so you saw the changes taking place—his face altered, losing weight rapidly, the expression becoming sad and fatalistic; he stopped changing his clothes, they got visibly dirtier by the day; his hands were marked, covered in spots and sores.

Then he'd vanish for a few weeks and you'd meet him again, fatter now but in a pasty kind of way, flesh that he'd put on during a period in hospital or perhaps in prison. He'd be trying to score again—but would tell you he was cured. There were a very large number of addicts like this and I found a lot of them hard to relate to, because so few seemed to have any awareness of what was happening to them at all.

Those junkies I knew who seemed to be pursuing a junk path and had some understanding, even a hint, of where it was taking them I could identify with. What was crushing was to see people falling apart who not only didn't really want to fall apart, but who didn't even know that they were. The suffering became meaningless, horrid, a bad joke.

There was no freemasonry amongst addicts. There was too much need. If you could keep the need within bounds then you could afford to be friendly to people; if it got out of hand then almost anything went—you had to get your stuff. My need was within some sort of limits so I didn't hustle people; but I wondered how long it would last.

Away from people's pads there were no real junk centres. Smack wasn't a public thing and apart from a very few places where you might be able to score, most of the network tied together in private houses. Junky places tended to be solitary scenes where you could turn on and groove quietly, places with a loo, certain record shops, hotels with elaborate lavatories and big lounges, sauna baths and rock clubs where you could cruise in your own head between fixes.

If you wanted to meet another junky in public—and you tried to avoid it—the place had to be well chosen because a habit stopped most people turning up on time. So it had to be somewhere you wouldn't be noticed hanging around for two hours or so, waiting. As often as not one of you wouldn't show anyway, having forgotten all about the meeting or got hung up with a troublesome fix. Until a beginner addict got into that rhythm himself there was a lot of frustration around.

I was getting into that rhythm and wondering about controlling it again. Most mornings I woke up and felt a flash of regret before taking that first fix, a hint of life escaping before it was lived. I made some casual and preliminary plans to go down to my parents' place in the country and cool it for a while. Then I'd see how I felt. But I put it off for the time being—with junk you can put it off for ever and never realize the years have gone.

Gerry had already tried to get off. He'd been to Morocco to give it a break and had returned, shattered. He came to stay at Gloucester Road temporarily and within a week of his return was using two or three grains a day. The weight had vanished from his frame; his eyes were large and staring and he looked constantly unwell, unable to eat properly, shooting coke all the time, sleeping in short bursts.

Even Max was having trouble. He, too, had returned from Morocco but with a habit still; and he was involved in an insane magical battle with two witchcraft freaks who had something against him. He took to sitting on Spike's bed for large parts of the day, needle in arm, occasionally calling out to the rest of us: Is it there yet? Is it there? This referring to an evil symbol which his enemies were projecting onto walls to obsess him. But Max would be all right, I felt, he was a survivor. . . .

One morning I woke up feeling worse than usual, the squalor from the latest four-day marathon strewn about me as I sat on the bed getting a first fix together. Annette's face looked troubled in her sleep beside me, vulnerable and isolated. Walking into the next bedroom and seeing Spike slumped out in an armchair, weak and breathing heavily, Clare unconscious on the carpet, a tourniquet still wrapped loosely round her arm, the television on from the night before, hissing quietly in the corner. . . .

The flat stank of destruction. I made myself some coffee and took it out onto the balcony to escape the atmosphere; drank it gazing at the passers-by in the Gloucester Road, normal life under the thin December sun. It was winter 1964, I'd been registered five months and was feeling the cold. And a hint of that old, deep fear.

I made it quickly back to the bedroom, rang my parents and accepted their invitation to spend Christmas with them on their farm in Wales. Throwing on some clothes I decided to go straight away while the impulse was with me, afraid I might change my mind.

I wasn't telling Doctor Robert that I might come off in case he refused to take me back—I wasn't that confident that I wouldn't need him. I asked for several weeks' scripts to cover me whilst I was away and wished him a merry Christmas. He looked doleful. One of his boyfriends had just left him and he was expecting to be lonely.

Annette was touring over Christmas. I said goodbye to her later that day and told the others in the flat where I was going. Then I caught the night train to Carmarthen.

In the train the junky syndrome began to operate: I would be off stuff soon so for now I could indulge myself. After eating I opened my suitcase, took out the bottles with thirty grains of each in them and settled down in the sleeping car to fix all night, my head lolling against the wall, the works in my arm, watching the darkness, alone with myself, the rails nodding me off into a stupor.

My parents knew about my addiction. After a brief panicky attempt to talk sense into me and persuade me to go straight into hospital they had left me alone, hoping it wasn't as bad as they feared. Little was said about junk when I stumbled off the train, stoned. It was almost Christmas and they were glad to have me home.

I set myself a withdrawal routine. I was using an average of two grains a day when I arrived, excluding the orgy on the train. I decided to cut it down by half a grain the first day and then by a pill daily. The result was immediate farce. I felt the nagging need for a fix all day long, even straight after taking one. The first day ended with me using rather more than two grains.

I did slightly better over the next couple of days but couldn't get the intake below about nine pills. And the stress of fighting with myself all the time for such a tiny result seemed more of a drag than abrupt withdrawal. Late in the evening, staring depressed at the junk bottle in front of me, I decided to try and get it over with. I tipped the bottle into a glass of water and threw it down the sink before I thought better of it.

Junk sickness is hard to describe, it takes a lot of different forms. I woke up the next morning with the early symptoms, running nose, sweating, weakness, and lay on the bed all day as it got worse. I never really got used to withdrawal but it was worse this first time because I never knew when it would bottom out or if it ever would.

The body disintegrated. By late that first night I had the lot: acute diarrhoea, inability to eat or drink, constant vomiting, inability to urinate, absence of sleep or rest. And the central symptom, a vague, indefinable hurt, somewhere between an itch and a pain, located in the viscera, as though every cell and nerve ending was rubbing against its neighbour. The reaction is the same in most people—you draw your legs up to your chest and bite your knees.

It peaked about the third day, and by then I was freaking out. The desire to get something into my bloodstream was overwhelming, anything to pull the organism together, to stop the fragmentation, to rest. I'd spilled some pills on the floor when I first arrived. Now I groped comically under the bed until I found what I swore was half a pill and made it to the bathroom to get some water. Deep down I probably knew it wasn't junk but I made it up anyway. It wouldn't even go down the needle properly and when I drew the blood back, instead of mixing with the murky solution in the works, it hung thickly at the bottom.

In a pathetic state, half in tears, I tried to force the plunger down as hard as I could until, with a loud report, the needle burst off the end of the syringe, drenching my face, hands and the bedding with blood. I ceased to care any more and lay on the floor watching the blood course out of the syringeless spike in my arm until it gradually clotted. And then I was sick again where I lay.

That was the nadir, when I gave up. The next few days passed in a haze I no longer remember. Eventually I slept by injecting barbiturate capsules into the muscle; after that things began to improve. I began to feel better, was able to get up and was finally left with a residue of minor symptoms that refused to go away, an acute over-sensitivity in my skin, the roof of my mouth, my eyes. My body was a foreign object, a misbehaving burden.

I stayed quietly in Wales, taking a dog out shooting, walking down to the beach, sitting in the open air, occasionally going out with my parents. But I already knew that I wasn't going to stay off, wasn't going to give myself time, if it was time that was needed. Life was empty and meaningless without junk. Now I was off I had nowhere to go. Constantly depressed within, I stared at the normal life around me with distaste and oppression, the rigid, chapel-bound existence of the Welsh, the poverty, watching the old men coughing their way to work in the quarries over the hill.

I was bereft, a part of myself seemed to have been ripped out; I had lost the sense that I knew where I was going, I knew I'd lost it and was scared of the implications. The true dimensions of the hook now became apparent, in glimpses, before I closed my mind to them. I was attacked for the first time by the feeling that I was playing a part in an unknown drama where none of the rules or the plot was made clear to me. The feeling vanished as quickly as it came.

Annette phoned not long before I returned. Was I off?

'Yes,' I said, 'I'm off.' She was delighted, of course.

'Is everything all right?'

'It's a bit more complicated than I expected, that's all.'

I took my mother to Midnight Mass in the little Catholic church in Carmarthen. She was happy, believing that my problems were over; I was sad and upset, feeling I had failed, afraid to tell her the truth in case it hurt her too much. I never found a way round the conflict. From then onwards I ceased contacting my parents, aware that any news I had for them about myself would be bad. To meet them was too hard, thinking of myself as a standing reproach to the efforts they had made, a sense of inflicting gratuitous pain. Very occasionally I was to visit them in the future; but the atmosphere, however hard they tried, was one of unease and worry.

On the way to the station I called in at the local chemist's and picked up the three weeks' scripts that I hadn't used. Once I had the gear in my pocket I still didn't want to fix it and sat in the restaurant car staring out of the window, looking out at the Atlantic where the line skirted the shore, feeling nothing inside, a void. I had my junk and didn't want to take it.

And I couldn't live without it.

5

I was fixing again within an hour of being back in the flat. For a short while I kidded myself and stalked about the room with a spliff in my mouth boring the others as I told them how great it was to be off, even though I might try a taste. Finally my speed evaporated and I started getting bottles out.

'Thank Christ for that,' said Gerry, reclining on a settee. 'If you'd gone on like that much longer we'd have thrown you out. All this high energy buzz. Unbearable.'

I got a quick hit and the junk flooded into my veins, warm, warm. What had Charlie Parker said? 'I see my heart specialist, I give him a hundred dollars, he treats me but it don't do me no good. I go to this ulcer man and give him seventy-five dollars to cool my ulcer out and it don't do no good. There's a little cat in a dark alley and I give him five dollars for a bag of shit—my ulcer's gone, my heart trouble is gone, everything gone.' That was how I felt then; everything was gone. For the moment.

There'd been some changes whilst I was away. Clare's health was collapsing again and Spike was screwing things up, not going into the office, staying home and fixing all day. There was trouble with the company. The American agent had ripped off all the US takings—one million dollars—and it looked as if the business couldn't survive without the cash. There were hurried consultations the first few days I was back with various solicitors and accountants descending on the pad. We divided them into two groups: those who were hip and the others that you had to prepare for by hiding all the works.

Gloom permeated the flat. Max was in trouble again: the Danish girl he'd recently married had got it into her head that he was trying to drive her mad. She'd refused to come back from Copenhagen and Max was preparing to pursue her, certain that someone or something had brainwashed her and turned her against him. He bought a new car within a few days of my return and set off for Denmark, leaving the business worries behind. All of us seemed to have overstepped the line at the same time. Spike and Clare copped out and went into West Park hospital together, leaving just Gerry and me in the flat. I was prone or stoned trying to keep that warmth; Gerry was building up an enormous habit at top speed, spending most of the day sitting on a bed in a semi-foetal position, either making up a fix or putting it in. For the time being I didn't think about being hooked at all. I was so glad, so relieved to be able to fix away the aches and pains of being off.

I had about a hundred grains of heroin spare—the stuff I hadn't used whilst I'd been in Wales. Trust with junk and one's friends goes only so far, especially when there are lots of visitors. I spent an evening cutting the centre out of a book and sealing the smack into it: that way I could sleep more easily at night. During the next few weeks I sold small amounts of it and kept the rest in case of escalation.

Once I started using again the habit went up very quickly. Within ten days I was fixing more frequently than when I'd left town. I was on a precarious point of balance. Having just screwed up a cure I had no illusions to keep me going; but the junk was providing a temporary screen against the future and worry. I had a simple reality: turn on.

But it obviously wasn't going to continue that way and I knew it. The atmosphere around me was funny, it was as if there were storm clouds building up all round the flat which were not visible from within. I waited unthinkingly for them to burst.

Gerry was in a similar state, although it was hard to know what to make of him any more. The changes hadn't been all one way. He'd somehow become more human since getting hung up. Previously there'd always been his frantic, hard movement, his evasion of contact; it was always flee or exploit. Now most of the speed had gone and a lot of the hardness with it. He had always been self-sufficient: now he needed people, doctors for scripts, other junkies when the gear ran out or a panic was on. And he liked it. Junk took him out of the power game.

But it was a chancy humanization course and anyone

observing us at the time, Gerry on the bed or watching television through glazed eyes, me stoned and silent, might have wondered what the benefits were. Neither of us seemed to *do* very much and with Annette and Clare away there wasn't any feminine influence to stop the flat falling apart. Occasionally I would search for a snort of coke to get me moving to clean the pad. It was usually gone, burnt down by Gerry who now had a mad cocaine habit which left him big-eyed and twitchy.

Spike and Clare appeared late one night, on the run from West Park and wanting a fix. The drug unit, like most drug units, didn't have much idea and their treatment had been unpleasant and erratic. Clare looked much better, like most women after they stop. Like me they were desolate without junk. But they couldn't stay out; Spike had developed an abscess on his lung and needed treatment.

We gave them all the gear they wanted, waited till they were stoned and suggested that they go back to hospital. They would have to be away for a long time to have any chance. Spike asked me if I wanted to take the flat over. As he owed around five hundred pounds rent I declined and rang for a taxi to take them to Doctor Robert's.

Notice to quit arrived shortly afterwards but we sat it out, neither of us wanting to do anything positive about finding a place to live or anything else. By now I was starting to crack. The screen that junk had provided for a few weeks was splitting open and I was feeling the cold again. A numb, despairing feeling began to overtake me; there was just nowhere to go, not backwards, not forwards. I began to get the horrors again.

Maybe I had it in my hands to alter things, to try and avoid the blind alley I was running into, but I doubt it. The one course of action that I didn't even consider was another attempt at stopping; there were too many reasons why it couldn't work and they went deeper than I suspected even then.

One Saturday morning the landlord arrived to take possession. Annette was there that weekend, as was a friend of hers who'd been making an intermittent scene with Gerry. It was nine in the morning when the man arrived; Annette had just got out of the bath and was walking, naked, into the bedroom. I was finishing a fix. I looked up with only moderate interest, satisfied myself that the fellow, a big man in a camel hair coat and hornrims, wasn't the fuzz and went on with what I was doing. He blinked, paused, stared at the two of us and walked on into the living room with his sidekick. Gerry and Rosalind were lying, also naked, on the floor.

I had to laugh. The landlord blew up. But it was bizarre the way he picked on one aspect of the scene. He'd seen Annette and he'd seen me with a syringe in my arm. But he chose to ignore that and instead worked himself into an absolute fury over Gerry and Rosalind and their immoral location on the carpet.

'On the floor! I have people copulating on my floor! Get out of my flat. On the floor!'

And while we got dressed and tried to cool him down he kept returning to the subject, being almost affable to me when I reasoned with him but still beside himself over the other two.

I agreed that we should leave later that day after a long hustle over what could be taken out of the flat—for the landlord had a court order and a warrant to seize Spike's belongings. Most of our stuff was excluded. As I was talking I suddenly remembered Max and his sixth sense for trouble. Before he left for Denmark I'd noticed him coming and going a number of times with cases. I'd taken it for normal travel preparations. Now I looked round and observed that there was nothing whatsoever of his in the flat.

The landlord departed, shaky and agitated. As he was leaving Gerry came out of his bedroom and triggered him off all over again. His aide ushered him out of the door.

The four of us packed some things and moved into a local hotel until we could get somewhere else. Annette returned after a day to her company; Gerry and I continued where we'd left off at Gloucester Road, hanging about the hotel room and burning down room service. Perhaps we were careless as well.

In any case, at eight-thirty in the morning after we'd been there a few days, there was a knock on the door and I found myself facing the police. My reaction was one of surprise for I couldn't think of anything I had done wrong recently. But they had a search warrant and turned our rooms over. A bottle of cocaine was found in Rosalind's handbag (she'd been tidying away after Gerry, she never used gear). And they found a history book in my drawer with ninety grains of smack in it. We were trooped out to a police van—past the rat-faced and incompetent bellboy who I assume had been going through my belongings looking for something to steal when he'd found the book and blown the whistle.

Chelsea police station and hard to explain. Where did I get all the heroin? From my doctor. If it was legal why keep it sealed up in a book? I agreed it looked bad. But I knew there was nothing they could hold me on unless I upset them. I sat, resigned, in a cell while they checked up with doctors and chemists at the law's slow pace.

As registered drug addicts we requested our rights to the drugs we possessed, and the police doctor was sent for. He arrived, mouse-like and scurrying, nervous and high-voiced. I was to remember that doctor but I didn't remember him well enough. We were taken into the charge room for junk to be taken under supervision. I quickly popped a small fix, more to break the monotony than because I needed it. Gerry, perhaps with premonitions, made a meal out of his.

Observing that the doctor didn't know much about junk and lacked confidence, he persuaded him to hand over all his prescription and made up an enormous dose. It was probably the largest fix he'd ever taken and he swayed about the room, unable to see almost, while the fuzz exchanged meaningful glances and the doctor looked on nervously, afraid that he'd blundered. Finally he collapsed into a chair and the doctor took the works out of his arm, signalling that we could be taken back to the cells. I didn't mind going back, having nothing better to do.

They unlocked us in the afternoon and told us politely that we were free to go, enquiries having established the legality of the gear. At the front desk they went through the routine of giving us our possessions back, one cop calling out the contents of a paper bag as he returned them, another ticking them off against a list. I got my things and waited for Gerry. It was sunny outside and I was itching to leave that police station atmosphere, a compound of disinfectant, linoleum and staleness.

'. . . one wallet,' droned the desk sergeant, 'one cheque book, one packet of cigarettes, one bunch of keys, one cheque book. . . .'

Two cheque books? I looked at Gerry, standing there deadpan as usual. So did the CID man at the next desk. His luck didn't change. He'd been talking to a kite-artist back at the flat a few days before and must have got hold of the other book then. So they took him away again.

There was nothing much I could do. I hung around until Gerry was charged. He had no defence and didn't want a solicitor. Rosalind's parents came to pick her up, shocked middle-class number. I didn't wait to see how that turned out and split, collecting a look of loathing from her father as I went.

It was around midnight and a thin sleet was falling. I ducked and stumbled my way along Onslow Gardens until I reached Alison's flat. And Alison was in, with coffee, warmth and somewhere to stay. At first she asked me questions that I couldn't answer, shocked at my appearance, wondering what was happening to me.

'I'm sorry,' I said, 'it's hard to talk. I don't know what's going on myself, really.' After a few answers of that kind she stopped asking. Alison was hip; she used gear herself and she was content to sit by the fire with me, sharing the junk, turning on together in the dimly lit room. After an hour or two she went to get some sleep and left me sitting with the bottles laid out in front of me, fixing time after time and staring at the fire.

Much later she appeared behind me and put her hands on my shoulders.

'Come to bed. Get some sleep.'

'It's sick,' I answered, 'I can't sleep in bed, Alison. I have to sit in a chair and nod off.'

I was just coming apart. I hadn't had anywhere to live since the hotel bust and hadn't wanted to find anywhere. I drifted from one pad to another, sometimes with people I knew, often with strangers I'd met the same day. I was tired and desperate, unable to see the way. Not long after leaving Gloucester Road, I'd started waking up in the middle of the night, sweating and cursing to myself, filled with dread. Any time of the day I was seized by fits of panic, palpitations and nausea.

I walked away from people in the middle of conversations,

suddenly horrified and unable to bear contact. I'd taken to descending on Dr Robert in the middle of the night, asking for solutions.

'Listen, I keep thinking I'm dying. I can't sleep, I can't move, I can't do anything.' Each time he checked me over and told me I was sound. Then why the horrors? He could have told me that chickens were coming home to roost; but he said he didn't know and offered me tranquillizers, more sleepers and methedrine. And methedrine made things worse —a quick boost that left me too stoned to know whether I was up or down, then paranoia and disorientation, menacing shadows all around me.

Now I sat in Alison's, trying to grasp what was going on. Events had become a meaningless jumble. I was shaken by the speed at which things had taken place, by the way I'd fallen apart so quickly. A year since the first snorts with Gerry. I thought of Gerry, whom I had visited in Brixton a few days after his arrest. When the screw had led him into the cubicle I'd been stunned by his appearance: it was simply all wrong. His face drawn back, tight, stretched and yellow. He was unable to talk properly; the words had tumbled out unmodulated, the sentences disjointed. And his neck was twisted, his head angled to one side. No junk.

Nothing at all?

Three tranquillizers a day and anti-vomit pills. Otherwise nothing.

I cut the visit short because of his state; a few days afterwards I rang his parents to find out more. He'd collapsed, the mother told me, was in an outside hospital for emergency treatment, condition critical. I was the luckier one.

I got up to make some coffee, trying not to crash things over in the kitchen. Outside the sleet had turned into light snow, muffling all sound, glittering in the street lights below. I took the coffee, cracked open another ampoule of methedrine and went back to the fireside. Home was where the bottles were. I took two more heroin tablets out and dropped them into the ampoule, holding a match underneath to melt them down.

The ninety-grain stock I'd had was running down fast, lots into my arm and more sold around the West End, a couple of pubs around Goodge Street, the hippy cafés and coffee bars. That sort of clientele suited me; they were as lost as I was.

A stream of different faces, drop-out dealers, homeless guitar players, remand home runaways. Spider, the gentle faggot in denims with the tattoos on his face; Jill who wanted to sing and just got laid, Scott the mystic pornographer, little Mark and the others like him, with their copies of *The Holy Barbarians* under their arms.

I kept an inner distance from most of the crowd and they never knew what to make of me, finding me too far-away, snobbish and spacy. Spade William was the only one I'd dug—a sad affinity—and he was dead now, found the night before on waste ground in Soho.

William was a lonely little Jamaican, a gentle guy with a bad habit. For a while he'd found customers for me and I'd laid stuff on him in return. I'd last seen him the night before his death. Something had been building up inside him—the sort of desperation I detected in myself—and then he'd had a run-in with the police. I found him at the bar in one of the Goodge Street pubs with a few bruises on him, propped up in a corner. There was a chilling dullness in his eyes. I told him to come out to the lavatory and I'd give him a fix to cheer him up.

But something was gone; he was a tired man and at the end of his tether. In the lavatory he just murmured to himself that there was no point any more, no point at all.

'Have the fix, William, you'll feel better.'

'I'm not going to feel better.'

And I'd laid another fix on him before leaving in a helpless attempt to do something, feeling sure inside that it couldn't help. Nobody could help.

I banged in the methedrine speedball and felt myself moving up, wired out, part of the falling snow, cold, solid cold, inside. My mind ranged madly through visions of ice, the stars outside, darkness and space, distance—and death itself, the old enemy, now close and almost in the room. The solid shapes of the flat dissolved before me into a network of fine cold lines with me at the motionless centre. How long, I didn't know.

With a jerk I sat up, frightened again after the stillness. Too close, too much stuff. I got up and moved about the room, jerky and unco-ordinated. Wake Alison? Talk to her and make love? I couldn't. Grabbing her keys I made for the door and the street, feeling the need for fresh air before I passed out.

It was still snowing slightly. I padded along, looking behind me, feeling I was being followed, forgetting where I was. But walking provided a function, a discipline to counter the stream of chaos and misdirection in my head. I walked up to Knightsbridge, my footsteps a wavy, serpentine confusion behind me. Finally, tired out, I sat on a wall until the horrors began to ease. It was hard to go on like this. Teeth chattering, I started walking back to Alison's.

For a few more weeks I went on crashing at different places, attempting meanwhile to stop the downward slide from getting any worse. For a while I stayed with the mystic pornographer in Westbourne Terrace. Scott was a tiny guru to the young drifters who surrounded him and quite hip in his own way. He'd made blue movies very successfully for a couple of years. The trouble was he'd started using junk: and the more junk he used the more gross and futile making dirty films appeared to him.

He lived with a large Manchester chick—the Westbourne Grove type—who worked in Whiteley's and looked like a hustler on the side; she attempted to keep his feet on the ground and the money coming in. No good. The more he fixed, the less he worked. When he got stoned he tended to walk over and press his forehead against you.

'What are you doing, Scott?' I asked, as I stepped back.

'Put your head against mine, man,' he said, 'and feel the spirit.'

But there were too many losers hanging around Scott and I felt the need of a quieter environment. There were still a few straight people around I hadn't lost touch with, and I contacted one of them who shared a flat in Chelsea to ask if I could stay a few weeks. Or rather I turned up shivering at midnight on his doorstep. It was a big flat and I thought it would do me good to mix with non-users for a while.

In retrospect it was possibly unwise, especially as I wasn't really aware of the effect I could have on straight people at this time. An even stronger than usual atmosphere of destruction and imminent disaster surrounded me then. I had taken to wearing black clothes and dark glasses, and I felt very faint intangible, not really connecting with people on the material plane. Frequently I went into pubs and clubs where I was known and passed unrecognized or perhaps unseen.

At the flat it freaked them out. They were mostly my own age, at the start of careers as writers, artists or architects. They were amiable enough but I noticed (even in my unnoticing state) an occasional tension in the air. But then I wasn't very cool. Not realizing the effect my deathly appearance and strange vibe was having on them, I was sometimes tactless, a typical junky guest.

I'd met another user called Smoky who was in most ways a far worse sight than I. He was absolutely cadaverously thin, had long, lank, horror film hair hanging over his face, walked with a stoop and had lost all his front teeth. He was about the same age as me. On a tube from Piccadilly one night we sussed each other out and got talking outside the station. Smoky, who talked slowly in heavy cockney with a speech impediment, wanted to buy stuff. I had the gravest doubts whether he would live long enough to complete any deal; but he persevered and I agreed to sell him a few grains twice a week.

Most of the time I met him in places of his own choosing, which in my subterranean mood suited me also, strange Joe Orton locales, West Brompton station ticket hall, the public lavatory at the World's End, numerous filthy cafés in Fulham. But once or twice we met at the flat and the sight of the two of us, each in our contrasting ways looking complete messengers from hell, horrified the flatmates even more. What sort of people was I bringing back? They had respectable friends. . . .

I smoothed things over at first but Smoky posed difficult problems. He started fixing in their bathroom and, as was his habit, in the hall. That blew it. I decided to leave before they made a physical attack on me.

My last night in their company summed it up. I went with one of them, Nick, a nut-case whom I liked best, to see some friends of his. It was a potentially slick evening in Edith Terrace—with a trendy Chelsea practical joker and his *Vogue* modelling lady, long dark hair, velvet trouser suit type. We sat smoking grass with me making innumerable trips to the bathroom, returning paler and more intangible each time, hardly able to speak or respond to conversation.

Two more guests arrived, an appalling pair, the man an aging hustler in a blue and badged blazer, with thick gold rings and a sort of modified corporal's voice, the wife a bleached forty-five-year-old, erect and edgy. But the man was an amazing speedy raconteur with an endless supply of triumphal conning stories. I stirred enough to press more and more hash on them, unwisely perhaps as the man was already drunk before we started.

A pitch of confused hilarity was maintained until the hustler, having grown speedier and more manic by the minute, reached the climax of one of his tales, searched for the words excitedly, dragged at the spliff in his hand—and crashed, grunting and holding his throat, to the floor. A coffee table and cups tumbled after him.

I peered through my shades, Oh, no, I thought, not more lightning.

The wife took over and manipulated him onto a couch. A pall descended over the room, broken only by twisted noises from our friend. A doctor was summoned and Nick and I said our goodbyes.

'These things only happen when I'm with you,' said Nick as we stumbled away.

'It follows me around,' I replied. Nick looked glum.

6

Lots Road. The power station ran along one side, backing onto the Thames. Next to it lay a council rubbish plant where garbage was transferred from steaming heaps on the wharfside. Between the two there was a gap a couple of yards wide, giving two houses a sight of the river. Appropriately I moved into a house with a view, past the rubbish out over the water.

The initial fascination with junk was gone. Now I was trying to live with it. There were plenty of other junkies about on a similar scene; but already I'd seen too many of them trap themselves in the junk equation, leave themselves no escape route when it became too much. I was determined to avoid that. I was not to be overwhelmed. But that meant bending, like a branch under strain.

Disaster receded for a while. I stopped avoiding people, looked a bit less distressed and doomed. I was sleeping in bed again, not in my clothes. Spring was arriving. To celebrate I gave up methedrine. Much of the time I sat and wrote poetry. For money I started dealing hash again while continuing my deal with Smoky.

Smoky was a classic example of junk as the escape route, although at that time there were very few users from deprived backgrounds. He came from a poor family in Fulham, one of a large and unlucky group of brothers. One was an amphetamine addict, taking massive quantities of purple hearts and dexedrine every hour, always being arrested for theft and petty crime. Another brother had just got eight years for bank robbery.

Smoky seemed like the biggest loser of the lot. And yet. Somehow he had a role and even a weird sort of dignity that had escaped the rest of his family. Backward at school, hardly able to read or write, he was the one who had chosen a role for himself. A certain primitive cunning, doubled in value by its apparent absence, gave him survival power. Via junk he found friends and girls, money and a type of freedom. But a clue to the cost was provided by the way he moaned in his sleep.

It was obvious that he was using his cunning on me. At first I had supposed that he needed gear for himself and was too untogether to get more from his doctor; so I sold it very cheaply. But it became clear that he was buying and selling for a third party. I wouldn't have fancied being that third party, knowing how Smoky could never turn up on time, knowing his unawareness of others. I guessed that somewhere there was a junky getting sick very often.

I still met him in some odd places, preferring not to deal at home. At one of our meetings he turned up with an old woman on crutches, a friend of his, although he took great care to exclude her from our transactions. I recognized her as the woman I'd seen in the East End doctor's the year before—so that crowd had been junkies after all.

She looked sixty but couldn't have been more than forty. Dressed then the way she always was, a man's grey flannel suit with the trousers tucked into the woollen socks. When she spoke she was an articulate, educated woman. She'd been a nurse, had got involved with one of her female patients, been turned on by her . . . .

That was all I knew for certain. But the story went that it was a heavy lesbian relationship gone wrong, and that the girl had spiked her drinks with junk over a long period, getting her hooked that way. It might have been true. I used to see her in the West End after that, in doorways, talking to herself. That was Jill the Crutch.

But I saw as little as possible of the West End crowd at that time, avoiding the more depressing end of the junk spectrum. Annette stayed with me a few times; we were a long way apart and didn't communicate. I didn't want us to live together. Annette didn't know what she wanted, was in fact going through a horrid period of insecurity and doubt. At the time, obsessed by my own weakness with junk and aware that at least she didn't use, I thought she was the stronger of the two of us. I was wrong. And I was blind to the fact that she might need me, unable to imagine anyone in their right mind wanting to lean on me. She went back to conclude her tour.

For company I started moving around with a couple of sisters I'd met at a party in Beaufort Street. They were an interesting and very attractive pair, one blonde, one dark. One sang and the other was a painter, and they both made their money—and a bit of the sixties glamour—by working as waitresses in a Mayfair casino. I got to know the blonde one, Angie, first; both were introduced but her sister, Julia, loaded on smoke and whisky, cut short the relationship immediately after saying hello by falling down the stairs and passing into peaceful unconsciousness.

Angie was one of the most original women I've met but wayward, even by my standards. A crowd of music hustlers and record producers could usually be found close by, all trying to talk her into recording and letting them manage her career. Couldn't be done. She sang on impulse and exquisitely, usually to friends. Sometimes she'd show at the Troubadour to sing for a couple of hours before splitting suddenly. A romantic novelist's dream.

Her sister was the deeper and less self-destructive of the two, with an apparent balance that the other lacked and perhaps a greater capacity for love. I wasn't making a scene with either of them initially and that suited me. Neither of them had anything to do with junk, both of them were loosely tied up. Julia was living with one of the gentleman croupiers at the club—casinos were outdoor relief for the upper classes at that time—but the relationship was sliding. Angie had a thing about Doctor Robert, whom she knew socially, wanting to convert him to women, so she said.

That was it with Angie: she came out constantly with comments and attitudes that could have been filched from second-rate romantic sources—but apparently they were quite genuine. One never knew quite what to make of it. Her sister avoided all stances and stock positions and perhaps that was what attracted me to her. That, her beauty and—surprisingly—her common sense. For Julia was one of those rare women who are both open to all varieties of experience and yet keep a sensible perspective.

The three of us met Gerry when he came out of West Park, the cure unit the court had sent him to. He came back to Lots Road and after the girls had left for work that evening we sat and talked.

He didn't talk much about Brixton. In West Park he had

been treated reasonably but had been unable to make the break with junk. The doctors had warned him about the future consequences of using with his weakened kidneys and flimsy constitution, but he seemed unconcerned. I wanted to know how good the doctors were at curing people. What was the treatment like?

Nobody had been cured whilst he was in there. Spike and Clare had simply disappeared one day. Some patients had looked as though they might have a chance, given time, but he wasn't optimistic. They used a drug called apomorphine. Apomorphine was the latest in a long line of fashionable treatments, the basis for using it being essentially the good reports of one doctor and a favourable write-up by Bill Burroughs in the preface to *The Naked Lunch.* It seemed that Gerry's doctors knew about as much as we did and some of them were willing to admit it. That was no use to me; I wanted people to fall back on who knew a hell of a lot more than I did. I began to suspect that there might not be any such doctors.

They also had deep narcosis treatment, added Gerry, whereby they put you to sleep for a week or two until the withdrawal had gone away. How did that work? Gerry laughed. You woke up as sick as when you went to sleep but two weeks older.

He'd persuaded the hospital that he was as cured as he was going to be and should be released. The doctor had signed him out saying: 'I'll be seeing you again, Gerry, as I'm sure you know. In bed or on a slab.'

'It gave me the creeps,' he added, 'like they had a lease on my body that was going to run out.'

He didn't manage to get cured but he bought a solid case of hepatitis out with him. He stayed with me that night and I was kept awake by incessant scratching as his skin showed the first signs of the disease. He was admitted to hospital the next morning. The guy still had no luck.

Another depressing episode. The sisters and I used to visit him most days and it was hard to know whether to laugh or cry. He was on the critical list and his parents were visiting him all the time, hoping that he wouldn't die. He was quite conscious, which as things turned out he rather regretted, and they let him have his gear. But what a drag! There was no shadow of communication with his parents at all, and written on their faces was complete bewilderment and fear. Every afternoon we'd walk in from the sun in the Fulham Road; every afternoon the parents were sitting there staring at him, always silent, occasionally weeping.

By the end of the week he could no longer take it and began to dive behind his screen at frequent intervals 'to give samples'—in reality to get stoned out of sight of the relatives. Julia and Angie would slip him hash to help him out.

But he recovered, a faint image of the person he'd been the year before. I moved to another flat in Fulham and offered to share it with him until he got some strength again, on condition he didn't scratch, I added.

A confusing game of musical chairs now took place. Rosalind, whose parents were still trying to make her a ward of court, was, I think, in love with Gerry and spent much of her time at the flat with him. Annette came back to stay for the last episode in our non-relationship. She had finished touring and we spent a few days being hard on one another before she announced that she was splitting for good.

Julia finally ended her scene with the croupier. Her sense of perspective failed her and she did it in style with forty nembutal. That was comfortably enough to kill her but she took them at Doctor Robert's, her subconscious possibly guiding her to a safe place. However, she nearly blew that as well, for Doctor Robert was drunk that night and incapable of diagnosing a car crash if he saw one. Later, on his way to bed and more sober, he realized dimly that something was wrong and called an ambulance. ('I kept trying to remember,' he said afterwards, 'small pupils, small pupils, what the hell did they signify?'). She went to Paris to recover.

And Annette moved into her place with Angie. Angie was bisexual, preferring women, and they made some sort of a scene for a while though Annette didn't like chicks much. They made a lovely-looking couple. I was used to being on my own.

But Fulham Palace Road was a blunder. The woman who owned the place and unfortunately lived on the premises let the flat to me thinking I was respectable. Gradually the scale of her error became apparent; we weren't going to be there very long. I had to be careful dealing hash and double-cool with Smoky, when he came, walking him not just to the street door to see that he didn't fix in the hall, but right up to the bus stop so that he couldn't turn on in the garden.

A stream of late-night callers and the occasional incriminating garbage were observed with mounting anxiety by the highly strung householder. The Polish wrestler who lived underneath disapproved of the noise. I started looking for another place yet again, attempting to mollify the woman with a long number about being a journalist and having to interview strange people.

Julia returned from Paris before I left and I gave a little party for her, off the cuff. The marvellous Max showed up early, together again, looking well and without a drug habit. He'd kicked in Denmark this time, amidst the ashes of his short marriage. ('She thinks I'm a fookin' moonster, Tony, terrified of my presence.') He was using again now, of course, but irregularly. And he had a new mad scheme that he wanted me to join. This time it was a commercial University Laundry Service.

'The key to this, mun, is that we only collect from the main gate or whatever these places have. The actual collection and distribution of laundry will be done by the students themselves.' He had a works in his arm by now and was striding excitedly about the room again. 'And we can clean up, to use a phrase, because those silly bastards will do it for a shilling a day. Can't fail, mun.' I declined to collaborate on the grounds that I needed my time and energy to devote to my habit.

Sitting there at night with my arm round Julia, watching Sandy playing his guitar, smoking grass and half-hearing Max in the background telling stories about his latest discovery, the drug LSD, to a group of disciples, I felt a momentary relaxation towards junk again. Perhaps it was possible to find a middle way, to take junk and drugs without disaster always at your shoulder, without losing contact again with others. Was there so much more that I ever wanted anyway? More than to be high, to listen, to be with people I dug? If one could accommodate things, be like the old mandarins, find a way to keep the habit steady . . . .

These illusions were curtailed in the crudest way when, in the middle of a fix, a half-inch spike apparently broke off and disappeared into my vein. I sat there sweating slightly, with a tourniquet round my biceps while others phoned for doctors, under the shadow of the junk cloud suddenly in the room. With some relief I discovered that the needle hadn't broken off but had slipped back into its neck like a child's toy knife. Calm was restored, externally but not within.

Later on: 'Tell me about LSD, Max.'

And he told me. How he'd discovered its existence from some friends of Timothy Leary, how taking it had led to the strongest and strangest experience since birth, how it had changed him over the past months. Summing up: 'I no longer know true fear and I have an idea where I'm going after physical death.'

Procuring the stuff was Max's scene exactly, for it existed in a never-never land, still legal but only obtainable after huge effort and conspiracy. A funny situation had arisen, reminiscent of the Rosicrucian Brotherhood (as LSD was in other ways), whereby a few tripped out doctors and scientists were travelling around Europe and the States, creating an elite market as a mission in life.

Acid interested me, but all the old problems arose in discussion, especially once Max had stopped talking and Sandy, whom Max had introduced to the drug, took over. Sandy was more typical of most drugs and acid users than Max, who had a solid kernel of protective sense and intuition.

' . . so there are seven atoms in the opium molecule and a corresponding seven in acid, and if you draw this diagram with seven corners you get the answer and the mystical connection . . .'

It was terribly difficult to talk sensibly about drugs and consciousness. So many people were unable to integrate their discoveries into their 'normal' selves without going ga-ga. You needed to be more discriminating and critical in your approach to what was real with drugs, not less. And while I knew for myself the reality of states that were outside normal comprehension and therefore accepted the validity of others' experiences, too often they became enmeshed in fantasy, unable to resist the temptation to relinquish all critical judgement. Inexplicable things had occurred, ergo everything was possible, anything could be inferred.

Thus Sandy, with his ramblings about discovering the secrets, his belief in unrefined occult theories, crude mysticism and numerology. And I certainly wouldn't have called

Sandy a fool—far from it, he was simply like a majority of people once they were exposed to other realities that they couldn't reject. I couldn't accept it; I wanted the sense at the heart of the experience, not flights of imagination and poetic interpretation. Something had happened to Sandy, something very important but it was being lost. Worse, acid had helped confirm his belief that he was on the 'right path'.

'But Sandy,' I said patiently, 'you're the best guitar player in England and you're still boring holes in your hands with junk. That can't be the right path for you.'

But we couldn't communicate on the subject. Possibly he took his musical ability for granted; perhaps it wasn't as important to him as it seemed from the outside. In any case he had faith. That faith, I reflected, was a dangerous commodity if you used junk: far better to believe the worst, that we were both simply fucking ourselves up. Nevertheless I wanted to try acid for myself and get closer to those areas that fascinated me. If they were real then they also had rules and pattern—however subtle—underneath the apparent chaos.

Then Max took over again, describing how he thought he knew the identity of the present incarnation of the Buddha, although he wasn't certain. In typical Max style his encounter with the Buddha had taken place in the lift between the tenth and eleventh floors of the Istanbul Hilton, where the Holy Man was staying under the guise of an English poet.

The party ended some time the next day, a few of us going off with Steve to watch him play somewhere on the South Coast. Steve was another princely musician who was taking risks with junk and other drugs, and also expressing an interest in LSD. But Steve also had a shrewd, hard core to protect him against self-mystification—although how long that core could survive in anybody was open to question. Later on he was gradually to become enmeshed as well, drawn after LSD to the study and practice of magic with insufficient caution, trapped by myth onstage and off, unable to discriminate between the forces he had aroused and pursued.

At this time he had adopted a very sinister and sexual persona for his stage act with mandarin moustaches, a sombrero and dark glasses. As we stepped, blinking, into the sunlight he spotted the nervous householder and in his kindly way sought to reassure her: he gave her a friendly pat on the bottom as he passed. Her husband looked on impassively. We were given notice shortly afterwards.

The musical chairs ended with Julia moving in for the last couple of weeks and the two of us deciding to get a place together. For both of us it was just a liaison at first, without a lot of thought for the future. Julia had her own aims and ambitions as an artist and was uninterested in an ordinary family life. The relationship deepened as time went on until what had started as an affair without any promises on either side became something much more permanent—and more complicated.

For in the long run, after the initial excitement and glamour had worn off, what was there for any woman in living with a junky unless she was an addict herself? Did one marvel at the faith and love of women in painful circumstances? Or wonder whether it was a vicarious identification through the man? I simply accepted it.

But Julia was in love with 'the man underneath' the junk, waiting patiently for me to give it up as soon as she saw where it was leading, underestimating, as most people did, the hold it was gaining over me. I came to wonder just who 'the man underneath' might be any more.

Gerry was still a sick man, but neither of us wanted to go on sharing and we had begun to get in each other's hair. He moved into another flat with Rosalind and we dropped out of one another's lives for a while.

Julia and I took a flatlet in South Kensington. A big house and far less claustrophobia. The best change of all was the housekeeper, a sweet lady of fifty who took a liking to us and talked incessantly while we moved in. After too many eagle-eyed householders that was what I dug; she had a prescription for dexedrine which kept her stoned, talking and unnoticing all the time. I was sure we would get along.

7

Ten in the morning. Julia still asleep beside me, late in from the night before. Did I have any gear left? I did not. A three-day prescription, I'd finished it last night. I got dressed quickly and quietly and walked out without waking Julia—morning was my own time, away in the magic circle of gear. It was a crisp summer day, just cool enough to prick my skin as I hurried to the chemist.

I was picking up regularly that summer from a little chemist in the Fulham Road, the sort of man who liked having some junky customers, liked to get involved with them and listen to their stories. He's looking up as I open the door, disappearing into the back of his shop where the scripts are kept, dispensing while I take a seat, stretching and yawning, waiting calmly for the stuff to be made up, knowing it's there.

I say hello to another user, one I know slightly, but not wanting to talk, not at this time of the morning; my senses are disarranged, my mind is on other things. I will talk to people later, I have only one object of interest at present. Then Mr Dale brings out my script, sealed up and ready, handing it to me with his ambiguous grin, half-colluding, half-reproachful. I pick up some syringes and split.

And a thin high as I hit the street with my package in my hand, my mind running even faster, tuned to the clangour in the street, the passers-by, the smells—of roasting coffee in the grocer's, of fruit and flowers from the shop next door, the scent of the street itself and—most of all—the clear cutting air as it hits the back of my throat.

A quick left turn to the toilets by the ABC cinema, I slow my steps for a moment to catch all the sensations one last time before I go inside and I see the sun reflected from the moisture in the gutters. Then a couple of shillings to the attendant so that I can have the locked washroom to myself.

Bottles, water, my mind is running in two directions, the fresh air outside, my target down here, what was the tension between them that fascinated me? A pause before hitting and then I am stretching out on the chair, reaching slowly for a cigarette. What had I been trying to think of just before I hit?

And the traffic noise outside diminishing, my heart, slowing down, I cannot hear the beat any longer. . . .

Then I was staring neutrally at my face in the mirror, taking a slow wash, examining the name moulded into the face of the soap. I could no longer smell the disinfectant, could be anywhere, a hotel, a bedroom, a street, it was all the same to me with my shortened focus.

And no more sensory overload—I was in control of the input, filtered and balanced to my own level. But always there was that quick catch of sadness as I hit in the mornings, something I was always on the point of grasping just before I took off, a train in the distance, a leaf on the wind.

I shrugged my shoulders, tidied up, made it back to the pad, picking up some cigarettes and croissants for breakfast on the way, walking differently now, more loosely and whistling to myself. Almost every day, I thought, a strange little passion play in the mornings. In a sense the peak of my day had already gone.

A lazy summer. Deal some hash in the mornings, go out for lunch. Shopping, necessary and unnecessary, in the afternoon an art gallery, buy clothes, the Kings Road. An idle, mindless time.

Those months were the high-point of my *identification* with junk. My dose high but not out of control; an apparently stabilized user, I didn't feel pressed. Inverted heroism, the future written off and therefore a temporary, Faustian happiness. On a more healthy note I loved Julia, in my own way, and the security and warmth which that relationship brought made it easier to live, relaxed, in the present.

In spite of the warnings and danger—or perhaps because of them—I did romanticize junk and developed a *style,* in attitude, in dress and behaviour. I had found or slipped into a role, a purely junk role during which I hardly used other drugs at all. A role for the unbalanced egotist, for it was no visible role or style at all, an absence of anything people could recognize or make out, partly because it was an essentially esoteric pursuit, partly because one couldn't flaunt drug addiction—that would lead to trouble. Uninvolvement, a refusal to identify with others' preoccupations, a contempt for everyday life and struggles. A hint of ostentation in dark glasses and Herbert Johnson hats. . . .

Reading the papers, my vision blurring—stories of drugs in increasing frequency, the odd scandal, other people were getting into similar things, a curious world that would be . . . the paper dropped from my hand and I dozed off, stoned. The sun shining through the big Cranley Gardens windows.

Sitting in front of the Hi-Fi I'd bought, talking, writing poor poetry—I couldn't tie my shoes half the time, what made me think I could write poetry?—Julia immersed in painting.

The Kings Road. Who is taking what? The latest faces to appear. Tommy Chomondly, having made a fortune playing chemmy, is unsatisfied and is now getting into stuff. A confusion of cultures, he wants to be a junky but he still carries a rolled umbrella and calls people 'my good man'.

Alan is there with his beautiful blonde wife, Nicole, whom I haven't spoken to. A hit record behind him, he wants to spend his money on junk. Edgy and dramatic. I wonder if he'll last the course. . . .

Angie appears in the Kenco where I am sitting quietly, having just returned from the cloakroom. She is leaving for Rome soon, she is in love with another woman there, a married woman; there will be problems. I ask her lazily about Annette. Annette is living on her own now, just off the Kings Road, using, says Angie, a lot of pills. I make no comment.

Doctor Robert's surgery, and the doctor also mentions Annette.

'She's still fond of you, talks about you a lot.' But that's the fag in Doctor Robert talking, I think; Angie has told me a different story. But then the good doctor takes an active interest in the relationships of his friends and 'favoured' patients, the sort that leads to arguments.

'Have you thought about cutting down again yet?' he asks, as he writes the prescriptions. 'Four grains a day is really too high. Have you thought any more about hospital?'

'Like David Boyle,' I reply, referring to the latest victim of the deep narcosis treatment, 'but he never woke up.'

His face clouds. Don't be flippant, he is clearly in sentimental mood today.

'I was very fond of David,' staring over the the desk, 'and I'm fond of you, you know that.'

Try it on.

'I need to stabilize before I think seriously about it,' the words come out in the junky rush,' and I don't have enough now. Just another half grain. You must know I need it or I wouldn't ask. The worry isn't helping Julia—'

He reaches for his script pad again and writes rapidly, tearing if off and smiling me a goodbye in one movement.

Outside in the street I check the script, knowing that I don't badly need half a grain but wanting a safety net. He has given me sleeping pills. I tear the script up into small pieces and throw them into the gutter.

If I did run short then I could score at Preest's, first of the hip spades—a derelict basement in Notting Hill, but always spotlessly clean. Preest would be walking about in his short dressing gown, friendly and welcoming. Always a crowd of heads in the place sitting smoking, white guys usually, show-business people, the occasional model. A really ferocious Rastafarian with buttered hair would be walking around the joint keeping it tidy, a fetish of Preest's who would also spray the place with Airwick every few minutes to try to kill the smell of weed.

'You're using more, Tony,' said Preest as he sold me half a grain.

I hear Max is in Formentera for the winter, trying to get into property development there. Idle thoughts of joining him but I need the prescriptions, those four grains a day. . . .

And the mornings were cold now: I was grateful for the oil heater the attendant left in the washroom for me. I'd be shivering when I arrived, wrapped in a long coat, running the hot tap on my hands to make the veins stand up. Outside the crispness of winter air, breath rising in the street, what was I doing? A whole summer gone in a haze of junk. A catch of sadness and pain. But the traffic noise was diminishing, I couldn't hear my heartbeat, looking lazily into the mirror I saw the same face. Time for breakfast. . . .

Of course things were going on behind the mask. But the

inactivity of the preceding months only concealed the fact that I wasn't certain of my next move. Complacency was less the problem than the strange and unjustified belief that I had more control over the span of addiction than could ever be possible.

I had never been under the illusion that I wouldn't get hooked. But I did believe, vaguely, that I could 'see junk through', that the experience could be pursued to an unknown end in my own time. Whether that end would be disaster I was willing to gamble. But the gamble was really irrelevant, for junk had its own dynamic and one that would destroy my own conceptions.

Now I started to run out of time, the time that I had treated so casually, thinking that there was so much in which to experience and change. The junk dynamic began to speed up and carry me along at a pace that I couldn't comprehend, let alone control. Dimly I was aware that I had miscalculated. And what miscalculation! For I had got into junk like a baby and without a guide, thinking that I could deal with forces that were quite outside my vision.

At the deepest levels, the levels I hardly knew existed yet and could neither approach nor handle, elements were being liberated, destructive areas of the mind released that would normally remain in unacknowledged balance—if they were left alone. Pandora's Box. I had begun by confidently pursuing shadows. Even now I was still under the illusion that I had let a few creatures out on a lead; in fact the box was deep, the lid could not be closed and the forces were in full flight. So I brooded, partially aware of these facts but not, of course, seeing them clearly, knowing that I couldn't step off the train and faintly foreseeing a collision course ahead.

There was time to brood, for in January I went down with pneumonia, an illness with a fondness for addicts, and though I recovered fairly quickly I was bothered with a multiplicity of minor ailments and bugs, clearly related to junk.

And I needed more. Doctor Robert was sympathetic but unhelpful.

'But I can't possibly give you any more. We're all under pressure to cut down our prescribing, and besides what good will it do? You'll be back again in a few weeks.'

Doctor Robert was probably right. On the other hand I still had to get more smack.

So I had to start scoring regularly, at first buying half a grain a day over my script. As long as the amounts I needed were insignificant it wasn't very difficult, for I knew several addicts locally who usually had surplus. If anything went wrong with those connections I could try Preest and his Airwick. I could usually score enough for two or three days' needs initially, buying it with money I was still—though decreasingly—making from hash. If it got tight I could swap the small amount of cocaine that I was still prescribed and hardly used.

Sometimes I couldn't score and that meant the drag up to one of the chemists in town, Bell's for preference and Boots as a last resort. It was not just the squalor that put me off Boots in Piccadilly; there were always police about on the watch and the likelihood of getting pulled was considerable. And there were the occasional crooked or desperate users out to turn you over.

The commonest and crudest trick was to sell saccharin tablets instead of smack. As these differed slightly in shape and tasted quite unlike the real thing the trick was easy to detect. Success depended on paranoia—selling in the alleys around the Circus where things had to be hurried through in case the police turned up. It happened to me on a few occasions, but I was usually lucky enough to discover it in time and find the crook before he'd managed to score with the money.

Another deception was practised by Pam the Peke (she was a stylish whore from the fifties, Park Lane style, who always carried her pet pekinese with her) and was generally undiscovered. She got hold of heroin in twelfth-of-a-grain tablets and sold them as sixths. The tablets were very nearly identical; and Pam pulled it off by selling them apparently very cheaply so that people always scored enough to take big fixes which disguised the difference in strength.

There was a variety of other frauds, but these were mainly inflicted on people fresh to the scene who would fall for anything. The basis was nearly always the same: get hold of the money under any pretext whatever, score with it and think about the consequences later. People didn't mind being caught and knocked about very much—no-one could take the stuff out once it was fixed. But there was in fact very little robbery and violence involved in turning people over at this time—in contrast to the situation that developed in later years as supplies shrank.

When everything went wrong, as it sometimes did, I couldn't score the margin I needed and used up my three-day script too soon. Then there was nothing to do but get sick and hang around, loaded up with hash and a couple of sleeping pills if it was bad, until midnight when I could cash the next day's prescription.

Unlike the waiting time in Boots—sheer horror, sick, barbiturate ridden users falling about, rowing with the staff, police presence everywhere—Bell and Croydon's was still bearable; and the evening watch as addicts turned up to wait, pick up or score had a minor role in the junk subculture.

There one heard news of arrivals and departures, gossip and disasters as the users, sometimes as many as ten or fifteen of them, sat with their backs to the big fish tank. It was often preferable to go in after midnight when the rush had died down if one didn't want the gossip or exposure; but if I was sick I sat there, drumming my heels, from eleven-thirty onwards. I used to pick up and make it to the telephone boxes behind Welbeck Street, hastening down the road with the packages. Once inside, in the shadow of the old church, I turned on as inconspicuously as possible, coughing and spluttering from the slight sickness, an open telephone directory in front of me.

In the unlikely event of someone already occupying the box I was liable to get agitated, transformed from Cool Tony into an arm-waving freak, knocking on the door and inventing wild stories of dying relatives, major disasters, anything to get the bastard out of the way. Once I was in they could wait if they wanted; nothing would get me out until I'd straightened up.

Before getting a cab home I'd have a coffee and walk around the West End to see who was about, chatting to those users whom I only met in town. Moss would usually be there, stalking in the shadows. And Geoff—from the Swedish trip, so long ago— could usually be found after he'd picked up, spectral now, his face all cheekbones and eyeballs. He had a big habit, had been in and out of prison and hospital and was apparently resigned to being an addict for the rest of his life.

If it had to be Boots to score, then the only place to get fixed up in a hurry was the public lavatory underneath Piccadilly. More nightmares, grotesque West End faggots preening themselves in the mirrors, filthy stained walls, grunts and moans from the dossers and derelicts trying to sleep in the cubicles, the police opening the doors with master keys.

One night—not untypical—I found Smoky there and lent him half a grain out of the stuff I'd bought. He was in a bad way and had made things worse for himself, not only by his widely shared habit of using the toilet water to fix, but also by dropping his last dose on the floor after he had cooked it up. I'd heard a recognizable yell of rage above the other bedlam and a scuffling sound in the cubicle next to mine: that was Smoky sucking up the puddle of gear from the shit-stained floor into his syringe.

I told him to chuck it away and I'd lend him some. But he couldn't get that one in either because the police had climbed on top of another cubicle and observed the whole transaction, grabbing the evidence I'd passed over before Smoky could get rid of it. An unpleasant few hours in Saville Row police station. Informally I told them the truth about the situation and they dropped the case, either from lack of interest or because they thought I could change my story at a later date. Outside the station Smoky and I split up. I went to meet Julia at the club; Smoky vanished to fix the half grain the police had returned and also the syringeful of bacillus. He copped an arm abscess for his stupidity.

I had a fetish about clean fixes. Curiously those with fewer reservations didn't die of septicaemia so often as one would expect; it seemed that immunity could develop against some of the more common bugs. I had to give up using sterile water ampoules for a similar reason. As long as I used them all the time I was fine. But if I was caught somewhere and had to use tap water, I went straight down with a twelve-hour infection. Using tap water all the time there was rarely any trouble.

But the visible decline in others' standards was shocking to observe, the outer changes reflecting a corrosion within. To meet people who'd got hung up at the same time as myself was chastening; and the deterioration could be marked from month to month.

In those who did decline badly—a clear majority—the personality, perhaps the humanity, could be observed peeling away like the layers of an onion. It began early on when conventional standards of morality were found—quite appropriately—to be irrelevant to a drug-addicted existence. Then a gradual hardening of attitudes took place, an unwillingness to see others except as either instruments or hurdles on the way to junk. Then another layer, the layer of common humanity underneath the legal and moral being—its removal, or shrivelling, was marked by an inability to do anything at all for others even if the desire was still there. Later, honesty to the body itself was lost: filthy fixes, poor food, teeth and skin rotting. Amongst downhill users it was quite common to see an addict, nodding after a fix, picking idly at his skin with a hypodermic and leaving open sores on the body.

Others maintained themselves with only minimal decline, even when their dose was large. So it was possible to remain human. Or did everyone, I wondered, eventually go the same way? Most of the users I'd known had been pretty normal early on. Was there any firm centre in people that didn't vanish if the stress was great enough? I rather doubted if there was. And it was hard to be judgmental—even if I'd wanted to—for deterioration seemed to be based not on greed or innate depravity at all, but on need.

Moss, a shell, the owner of the property had disappeared. Spike, from Gloucester Road, with TB and a frame like coathangers and string, unable to converse except in terms of the past, dreaming still of Clare's inheritance that he would never be able to enjoy except to buy more junk. Jill the Crutch, lying in her Piccadilly doorway, hidden behind a pile of overflowing dustbins, making herself food in a gashed and encrusted can. . . .

And there was I, flitting from door to door, dealing to get my extra stuff, stonewalling questions about junk from Julia or anyone else, taking to bed for a couple of days now and then to cut consumption down, retreating into a cold cynicism and maintaining more and more distance between myself and most other junkies.

I preferred the company of Chelsea people to that

desperation; they used smack in smaller quantities and preferred methedrine, cocaine and other less manifestly destructive substances. Their naivety about drugs, their gradual submersion in the drug myth of the mid-sixties, was annoying but less painful than the disillusion of the purely junk scene. But a lot of them were simply at an earlier stage. . . .

I was a compulsive divider of scenes anyway; I didn't want to be confined to any one social matrix in spite of my inner identification with junk. Odd juxtapositions: picking up at Bell's and playing roulette at the Casanove before meeting Julia; fixing in the loo at a gallery opening, a childish frisson at the thought of meeting one of my straight friends at midnight by my phone box, the look on their face. . . .

Occasionally the wires crossed, as when I picked up a script with Julia's brother one night after leaving a party. He didn't know what the script contained. Gentle, sophisticated Patrick, who hardly knew me then, found himself suddenly drawn into a dream sequence as John Bell's was surrounded by police and all addict customers were mousetrapped as they left. An addict I'd known had been murdered the night before after leaving the chemist.

He found himself making statements and giving fingerprints 'voluntarily'.

'But, officer,' he said, bewildered after an hour in Marylebone Lane police station, 'I simply came past here on my way to another party.'

But wires were beginning to cross anyway. At straight parties young TV producers offered you joints, proud of smoking openly, anxious to discuss the relative merits of Afghani, Nepalese and Lebanese. I professed total ignorance on the matter.

With more and more references to drugs, covert or otherwise, in music and writing, an increasing number of commentators and gossip columnists started hunting the Kings Road and Bayswater, searching for the centre of drug culture. There was no centre to track down; so they were thrown back on invention. Swingers emerged. Jokey straight figures from the early sixties, photographers, tradesmen, stepped forward to be identified as leaders of the new wave, cutting their alcohol consumption and taking up the weed.

I was reminded of the Bob Dylan song, written at this time about parallel events in New York, and the refrain:

There's something going on but you don't know what it is. Do you, Mister Jones?

There was something going on but you couldn't make instant history out of it because it was too new. And in all the confusion as people tried to find out just what was going on with drugs, two quite separate movements got mixed up together, with unfortunate results. The use of drugs, up, down and sideways for subjective reasons and exploration—a chancy business that wasn't of wide application—and the simultaneous acceptance of pot among younger people for simple relaxation and intoxication: the two were temporarily seen as one; discrimination was hard to find.

But at least LSD was easier to get hold of now. One Sunday Julia and I copped some—poured on sugar cubes as it was then—and settled down in Cranley Gardens to take a trip. We sat and munched the sugar in bits and pieces; nothing happened for about three-quarters of an hour.

Then the acid hit with a bang. A series of waves starting in the stomach and flowing up to the throat and head. But they also seemed to flow into the brain itself; so that it was hard to distinguish between physical and cerebral sensation. I felt sick and buffeted by the waves, each time one arrived in my head the thoughts themselves felt overloaded, the senses succumbing. I couldn't bear to look around me for fear that seeing anything in the room would overwhelm me, like a bottle of fluid thrown into my brain cells.

The sickness began to pass and I opened my eyes. Perception had altered completely; objects caused an immediate emotional as well as visual response; the nature of light had altered, shimmering in waves of varying intensity. I had to screen one of the lights off for its yellow glow was dirty and painful; by altering the strength and colour of the light source I could make myself feel less sick, or more.

I looked at Julia and asked her how she felt. She had been going through the same scenes and was fine. But her face! It was dancing and changing from moment to moment, ripples could be seen crossing her features. When she spoke the ripples anticipated the comment; just before she said the words, so her face announced—among other things—the broad nature of what she was about to say.

Julia and I, like many couples, knew quite often what the other was thinking, and over the years I had learnt to read faces to a considerable degree. But this was ridiculous. Both of us were very speedy and wanted to talk a lot: before the other's words were out we were already responding. A few minutes of this and we started conversing in gestures and monosyllables, reading the meanings off, needing only occasional interjections for the most complex ideas.

But apart from this clarity of communication there was a lot of inner confusion. The alterations had been so extreme, the changes so fast and extraordinary that neither of us could quite keep pace with what was going on. We were both experiencing such a perceptual bombardment that we felt we were only just holding on, we might almost vanish under such a weight of impression.

The feeling of seeing things for the first time was very marked. Every object was seen to have its own essence; it gave out different light reflections; it caused a different emotional response. And there was a difference between organic objects, such as fruit and wood, and manufactured things like porcelain and glassware. The former had a greater intensity.

Colour sympathies were enormously magnified—colours that one had never been keen on became ugly and abhorrent; colours one normally liked now offered a deep glow of friendliness. And everywhere was the dominating power of light, shimmering, reflecting and scattering off into cloud-chamber paths and rays.

After a couple of hours the strength of the trip became too great for me to observe things coolly, and I was reduced to reacting to events rather than seeing them. And the deeper sensations and experiences were too confusing to be meaningful—at that time I lacked the words to describe them and the framework to comprehend them.

And fear took a hand, for I knew that in a crucial sense I was not ready to take acid. As the strength of the trip increased, so one was sucked into a spiral of thought and feeling, being drawn down deeper and deeper into unconscious strata. I knew later, and felt intuitively at the time, that this spiralling eventually reached a firm centre, a centre that provided strength to combat the fear that can envelop anyone who trips—the fear that perhaps the helix has no end and that one will descend forever into bottomless chaos.

I was oppressed with the fear that my centre was somehow subverted by junk, and that instead of arriving at a base of safety and acceptance, I was going to become screamingly aware of the tenuous state within. This feeling must have been based partially on my experiences of the year before, after my failed cold turkey, when the body had seemed about to give up in a cry of panic.

So my responses to the trip became inhibited. After something over two hours I therefore took a large fix—paradoxical as it might seem—for heroin has a slightly antagonistic effect on LSD. It certainly didn't bring me back to normal, but it prevented the trip from peaking at full strength.

Fixing was atrocious, the syringe vast and sinister in the flickering light, the feeling as I pushed the needle into my arm akin to butchering a baby and trampling on the corpse. The message came loud and clear.

Julia had taken less than I and was anyway essentially balanced within, overwhelmed but extraordinarily happy, her face apparently glowing with love. Feelings seemed to become tangible—perhaps one of the reasons why burnt-out trippers come back raving about the power of love. The feelings of potential chaos were always stilled by warm emotion; unfriendly feelings immediately had a horrible effect, sending one into a flat spin of loneliness and sorrow.

Later on a friend of Julia came round—stoned on something or other and therefore providing a slight bridge of communication—and knowing that she wouldn't be on her own I left to pick up a prescription. All events took on a simultaneously logical and symbolic value with acid, and as I stepped out into the cold wintry evening I was never more aware of exchanging the warmth of a woman for the hard rejection of a chemist. But, as I reflected at the time, exchange it I still did.

After a chaotic taxi trip—speed and traffic and silence, like a space capsule—Bell's looked like a death ward to me, brilliantly lit by icy fluorescent lighting. The fish swum mindlessly, gaping at me. I wanted to get out as soon as I arrived.

And the tension which had been mounting up blew out—I couldn't stand the place and grabbed my package and ran, old Mr Latimer at the counter probably thinking I was sicker than usual. Outside I was suddenly terrified, feeling trapped with nowhere to run to, my legs had turned to rubber and I was sweating. Traffic noise spooked me, threatening to envelop me completely, and passers-by had the faces of demons. The shadows in the doorways took on menacing life. I felt suicidal, hopeless.

But I walked slowly to the telephones by the church, reminding myself that this was an expected reaction and was bound to pass. Another Calvary in the phone-box—flesh mutilator!—and I began to calm down, staring into the little mirror, observing the way my face had hardened over the past year or two, the mouth turning downwards.

I checked the time: it was getting late. Still out of it I walked back along Wigmore Street to find a taxi. Not seeing one I cut through to the antique market, intending to walk to Marble Arch, pausing under a lamp post and considering the prospect before me. I could walk down to Oxford Street and along—but look at those weekend crowds, everyone of them would be monstrous in close view, and the noise. . . .

If I crossed the road I could walk down a side street and pick up a cab by the Cumberland Hotel. But the street was deserted and dimly lit, those shadows. . . .

The occasional passer-by saw me leaning against the lamp-post, probably taking me for a drunk, unaware that I had nowhere to go. Time was meaningless.

I felt the trip easing off, and as a cab deposited some passengers on the other side of the road I broke away and hailed it. Riding home, shattered as though I had been hiking for weeks without rest, I checked my watch again. It was one in the morning. We had taken the trip at two in the afternoon and I had been hung up at the lamp-post for three hours.

8

Spring and warm weather again. . . . The pattern of time . . . The framework of life breaking up and falling away . . . Three, four, five days a week scoring, searching for cheap junk and plentiful supplies . . . Shooting it up as soon as I got it . . . Money running down, no longer dealing hashish, neither the time nor the energy to spare . . . Time distorted, spurts of hyper-activity getting the junk, long periods fixing . . . Staring at the wall . . . Mosaic of unrelated events.

Seven grains a day to find. The train was running away with me.

'This is ludicrous,' to Doctor Robert, 'you're giving me about half my intake. I might as well not be registered at all.' But there were to be no more increases, just the occasional extra script if I looked sick.

Making the rounds of the other junk doctors . . . Wimpole Street, Wigmore Street, half a dozen strange surgeries . . . You mean you want more drugs, Antony? I stared at the woman; her desk had been designed to let her breasts fall onto the top, the maternal image . . . The odd emergency script to get me out of the surgery, stop me making a fuss. Caught in an impossibility: sooner or later all junkies wanted more of something than any doctor could give, the logic of the situation.

Thinking idly of a cure, a response to the pressure . . . Nodding off . . . I would be in hospital . . . But to what end? Could I believe I would stay off? No. Listening for changes within, messages to indicate something lasting, something more than a flight from hard times. There were none. That acid trip . . . Acid had shown up the conflicts and inner danger . . . But insight alone wasn't enough. Where was the will?

Dreaming at night . . . Pictures of myself: a shadow in a black jacket, running in and out of doorways and archways

... At bay, surrounded by Mafia hit men, by unknown assassins, by giant spiders ... Captain of a ship with no crew, smooth indigo seas, no land in sight. ...

Putting the light on to take another fix in the silence, Julia uneasily asleep beside me. ...

Fixing ten, twelve times a day, the buzz reduced to a fleeting sensation at the back of the throat ... And getting sick more and more frequently and insistently ... A few hours without a fix and my eyes are running, I can't see, too disorganized to think clearly . . . In Goodge Street one afternoon, so sick I fall through a plate glass window ... Anything to get out and away, a decreasing control ... Shooting morphine, cocaine, methadone, methedrine, codeine. Chewing tiny bits of acid, not enough for a trip, just to get out of my head ... Smoking opium ... Dropping sleepers every night.

Seeing less and less of Julia, inventing reassurance for her when we talk. Out all day, seeking out the few users who have enough to service my needs at the right price. A difficult crowd, but beggars cannot choose. So many of the dealers are so lonely, they invent reasons to delay the transaction, keep one waiting, a need for company. Or, occasionally, hard cases like Curtis, with his dark clothes and one gold earring, making his punters clean the flat up and wait on him before he'd hand over the junk—one visit was enough for me; I lacked patience and had to take it from him.

Pam the Peke. Pam was alone and desperate, a bad phase, stoned on methedrine all the time, unable even to whore—but plenty of cheap junk. The pilgrimage to her Kings Cross hotel almost every afternoon ... She had the gear stashed in penny packets all over the room before I arrived. At intervals she suddenly produced a handful of pills and offered them to me. Three hours was the average time to score from her, humouring her. But I always went back the next day.

After a month she decides she is in love with me. Now when I leave I am the recipient of verbal storms and thrown crockery, then the threats to kill herself and the occasional lunge for the razor. To get out at all I have to put her to bed as she weeps and raves, the methedrine sending her right over the edge.

She always wrote poetry. Now she writes it, unflatteringly, about me and quotes herself: I am the Ice Man—not just because I won't sleep with her—the Uncaring, Mister Come and Go.

'Get out, Ice Man,' as the door slams behind me. 'Go on, fuck off to wherever you're going, desert me now you've got what you want, you monster'—Crash! as another vase hits the door, then the screams and gurgles. I lean back against the door. All I want is to buy stuff.

One afternoon I arrive and find a guy in bed with her, fixing. A defiant smile from Pam. I feel a great weight leaving my shoulders, concerned only that the new face might use all the junk.

After that the pressure eased; Pam was losing interest. Fortunately she continued to sell to me, in her erratic way.

She had confessed the trick of selling twelfth-of-a-grain tablets in the West End. But in her confusion she mixed the twelfths and sixths up so there was always an element of mystery in scoring from her. Once, unable to score all day, sick and falling around, I found her late at night in Bell's. Seeing the state I was in she gave me the bottle to take what I needed. Ill and uncaring I made up a turn on in the chemist's, shovelling the pills in by the half dozen, wanting a huge fix and thinking they were twelfths. But for once Pam was playing straight and I blacked out in the chemist's doorway with the works in my arm, falling out on to the street.

A curious way to spend the time . . . Losing my sense of humour . . . Perhaps time is spending me. . . .

Leaving Doctor Robert's with a script for an extra grain after the usual stormy scene, I found Moss in the waiting room. Knowing that the doctor had got rid of him years before, I asked him what he was doing. He had come back to get cured.

'Cured?' Not callously but in some wonder, 'You?'

'I'm serious. Talked with doctors and people, social workers; they're helping me. Giving me a lot of encouragement.'

He looked terrible. If anyone should have been left to go on fixing in peace to the end, I thought, Moss should. Over the next few weeks, seeing him pick up at my chemist in the mornings, bombed out on sleeping pills and tranquillizers, cracking under the pressure of reduction, under the superficial optimism a strong hopelessness—gambler's last throw.

Staring at the wall . . . A gulf with Julia that I couldn't cover . . . I held back the more destructive side from her, but that side was in the ascendant, little common ground . . . Fears of failing her totally.

Such an effort to stay straight, put on a show . . . Washing, shaving seem almost a waste of time, a pretence . . . A strain to appear normal, getting tired of doing so. . . .

Nicole, a model, who had a connection for cheap junk, a beautiful creature with a lust for junk and a shrinking heart, more self-destructive than I was, with no thought for the future as long as she could get gear, her husband in prison for drugs; she was fresh out of West Park hospital.

No need for effort with Nicole—there was no-one I needed to protect here. I'd seen junk as a barrier to feeling: now it was a bridge. We made fixes for each other, getting excited at turning the other on . . . A weird scene, a drugged debauch—scoring, turning on, stoned, fucking with a meth-strengthened sexual appetite amongst the empty ampoules, dirty tissues and cigarette ends on the floor.

And arguments . . . Often about how much coke or meth she should take . . . Nicole on stimulants: not just paranoid but completely insane, worse than Pam. Kneeling with her ear to the wall, listening for Customs men, thinking I am a policeman . . . Accusations . . . I'm after something, I'm going to kill her, steal her Habitat furniture. In the morning, calm again . . . But a bond . . . Nicole knew me as few people ever did, without illusions. . . .

A small trip together. Sitting in the Walton Street flat, the white walls, the acid taking hold . . . She talks fast and brilliantly, no barriers, vulnerability, then floods of tears, despair, recovery: 'I must take a fix.'

But so cold . . . Visions of ice, the walls moving slowly, like glaciers . . . Nicole calm in the white light, stroking her arm, turning to me . . . Successive incarnations seem to cross her face, back through time . . . She comes on as the priestess . . . Only you know and I know . . . The walls are replaced by pure whiteness and the silence of space, an absence of breeze . . . A message I cannot resolve . . . The presence of death in the room, her face like a skull and I tell her I love her. . . .

But that was no love—not the sort of scene to last. We

exhaust each other, no exchange of strength, only drawing on the other. After some weeks it ends in a night of violence and lunacy, Nicole hysterical and smashing the flat up, me sitting on the edge of the bed not knowing whether to laugh or cry—neither of us knows what the angst is about. At dawn she takes off her clothes, sets fire to a new fur coat, flings it burning into the street below. I bail out and walk slowly home to Julia in the early sunshine, finding her in bed and asleep. She has started taking sleeping pills at night.

Into my chemist—Moss is lying on the floor, unconscious. The chemist's wife steps neatly over him, reaching up to one of the shelves. They are trying to help him cut down.

And a sunny evening in Wigmore Street . . . Running down the road to Bell's with an extra script in my hand . . . Laughing loudly as I run, aware of the absurdity of my whole situation . . . People in the sidewalk café lift their heads as I pass, wondering what the laughter is about.

This was not science. I decided abruptly and in a moment of lucidity that I had to get a cure whether I wanted one or not, that at the rate my habit was escalating there wasn't going to be enough gear in London to support me.

I had few illusions about staying off. Equally I could not see myself surviving for very long as things were; and the prospect of another winter with my tendency to junk-triggered lung complaints was unattractive. Time to think it out? But there just wasn't the time, I knew that now. And I also knew that the pattern I had fallen into, neither able to resign myself to stuff—and therefore ensure myself a sensible supply and less conflict—nor able to believe in abandoning junk, was resulting in a perpetual-motion self-destruct machine. Time to step off for a while.

Thus in my infrequent periods of common sense and reflection. Aware of their current scarcity I moved as quickly as possible to find a decent cure unit, somewhere reliable in the midst of the minefield of hope, ignorance and charlatanry which comprised the treatment scene.

From what I had been told, the best unit in either the state or the private sector was the Salter Unit at Cane Hill in Surrey. There an imaginative consultant had managed to get backing for a semi-experimental unit, patient-oriented and democratically run, operating within the main mental hospital but administered separately. Doctor Robert introduced me to the psychiatrist and after a couple of interviews I was offered a place for later in the summer, conditional on satisfying the other addicts as to my suitability and adaptibility.

This was a relief, but more important to Julia who had been waiting for me to take such a decision almost ever since she had known me, Julia who had managed to live with my lunacy and irresponsibility without completely cracking up, still working and providing a semblance of balance in our lives.

For now I was burning everything down, selling some of the few precious possessions we had, spending her money, selling junk to others if I could score it cheaply enough . . . Thirty pounds a week to find, every week . . . Ten grains a day by June. What savings we'd had vanished.

The money can always be found for junk, however much is needed. More corrosive was the pressure. And I was through with that type of pressure, through with trying to get more out of Doctor Robert. I decided to find another doctor and get registered under a false name, illegally of course; but it might take a long time to detect. By the time they caught up with me I hoped to be in hospital where they probably wouldn't proceed against me. Anyway I felt that I had little choice. The same week that I got the hospital admission date I scored a large deal of smack from a smuggler and, freed from the need to hustle for a few days, I set out to get registered again.

Too many of the London doctors knew me, from giving me emergency scripts, from acting as Doctor Robert's locum or from throwing me out of their surgeries. But I heard of a new arrival, someone just starting to prescribe who was known to be willing to take anyone on without difficulty. I found his address and went along to see him.

Unpleasant. Whenever a new doctor appeared on the scene he got a rush of patients, either rejected by other doctors or double scripters like me. This was the worst I had seen; I recognized at least ten junkies who were known to be trouble. And there were another twenty or so I couldn't place, youngsters and hard cases.

Getting on with him was no problem. He was a little

fellow, nervous with funny eyes behind thick glasses. I thought I had met him before but couldn't be sure. I gave him the false name and address, told him how much I needed and waited while he wrote down a few details, mostly, I noticed, about identification features—a point that made me uneasy.

'I'll take some more particulars another time,' he said hurriedly. 'Come back this time next week. And that's two pounds please.'

'Cash?' I asked foolishly.

'Oh yes. And I'm afraid you must pay me every visit, otherwise I can't do anything for you.'

I gave him the money. He pulled open the drawer in his desk and dropped it in. Perhaps a hundred pounds in crumpled notes already lay there.

I made my way out through the bedlam of the crowded waiting room. Apart from the discomfort I felt at having broken the law in such a crude way, there was something else, something suspicious about the whole set-up that I couldn't put my finger on. But I had the junk I wanted and I dismissed it from my mind. Times change . . . It was certainly a very businesslike and logical way to get junk.

So, for a while I no longer needed to score. But the other part of the plan, the hospital bed, was delayed again and again; the balancing act was going to be hard to sustain for long.

We moved into a flat in Cathcart Road. I couldn't get it together to furnish it properly; it was spare and barren, an atmosphere of transit. Julia went on taking her sleepers at night, more worried than I was—being more realistic—about my getting caught for the illicit scripting. As the weeks dragged on and I still couldn't get a vacant bed things began to look a little insecure. There was a wasps' nest outside the flat and at night the creatures flew up at the badly curtained windows, tap, tap . . . harbingers.

Fixing . . . Avoiding straight people . . . But at least there was gear to spare . . . So many people getting into methedrine, like dealing with mental patients.

Meth was such a disaster. It had been considered fairly harmless until recently; now there was a lot in circulation. I never knew why, for it was in no sense physically addictive . . . Doctors went on churning it out . . . I didn't like the drug very much, partly because it made me physically uncomfortable, partly also because it was the most unliberating drug of all, giving an illusion of heightened reality, but in fact utterly distorting the sensory apparatus.

Others disagreed. Now it was becoming fashionable amongst junkies and drug heads generally. One walked into a Chelsea flat and was confronted by groups of people who looked as if they were wired into the electricity mains. The drug had a ridiculous effect on nervous co-ordination, making people jump and twitch like puppets on a string. And they were always hung up on stupid tasks—cleaning windows, dismantling machinery and talking excitedly . . . Talking such shit all the time.

It was getting like Sweden in 1964 with all the preludin floating around. King of the London scene was Joss, a withered and angular gentleman of means, holding court in Cheyne Walk, surrounded by freeloaders and disembowelled adult toys from Harrods—adding machines, electronic clocks, stereo sets. There a conversation about clothes or food or digging roads would go on for four days interspersed with the sound of breaking crockery. Joss disappeared now and then to the top of the house to dress up in drag and perform in front of the mirror. See one meth scene and you've seen them all . . . And the cosmic paranoia—intelligent people discussing the plans the government had for enslaving the populace, microwave stations were being built to destroy us, they were closing in. . . .

And given time and enough meth your head started to go for good, clouded and burnt by too much amphetamine, synaptic gaps frizzling at the ends. . . .

A waste of time.

Still, I wasn't such intelligent company myself at that time—more than a little paranoid, though not from methedrine, trying to remember to take the scripts to different chemists—wouldn't do to present two names in the same place—stripping the labels off the bottles as soon as I got them. Stuck in Preest's one night when the fuzz raided the place, two lots of prescriptions, two lots of junk on me; but I wasn't throwing them away. A motor cyclist crashed outside the house and I got away in the confusion, melting into the Portobello Road.

Doctor Ritchie's surgery . . . Any pretensions to a medical

practice disappearing fast: junkies sitting on the steps outside his house, sprawled all over his garden. More and more working class addicts . . . They came from the new towns and the big estates—potential for a hundred sociology articles there.

I now remembered where I had seen the doctor before—he was a police surgeon.

'Strange isn't it,' mused one of his 'patients', 'like you'd think the fuzz would be unhappy about one of their doctors making so much money from junk.'

And he was making money—thirty or forty patients any day one went there, two or three pounds a time. Later on, after he'd suddenly closed down, he made a donation to Cane Hill—three pairs of running shoes. Not that I was complaining; I understood the language of money far better than the language of 'help'; if money was all he wanted it was the easiest thing to find.

Of course, the police might not object if there was something in it for them. Doctor Ritchie acted like a magnet for all the most dishonest and desperate junkies in London. It was clear enough, but I didn't care very much.

Still no hospital vacancy, delay after delay . . . still the chemist in the morning. My last view of Moss, fading away, standing in the chemist with a bunch of flowers for the owner's wife. His hands were sweating and agitated and the flowers were breaking up, a mounting pile of petals at his feet. He mumbled a few words to Julia and myself. Julia painted his picture that day, overcome with the symbolism. It was all over; he hanged himself in prison a few weeks later, his last chance gone. No words to say. . . .

And Annette. Walking out of Doctor Robert's, I found her sitting in the waiting room, nodding off over a magazine . . .

'I'm waiting for someone,' she said, hardly seeing me, smacked out and glazed. I left quickly, shaking my head. . . .

The police came for me at the end of October. I was out but they had a search warrant and turned the place over, finding an ampoule of methedrine in a drawer. As an incentive to my appearance they decided to charge Julia with possession of the amp.

There wasn't really anywhere to run to. But I found it hard to accept the prospect of a cold turkey in Brixton—ten grains a day, and two years since I'd been off, a difficult case for abrupt withdrawal. Curtis had been the most recent casualty, left to drown in his own vomit in a cell.

I prevaricated for a day, avoiding the police in the chemist's, staying with a friend who had nothing to do with the junk scene—and fixing. Julia was bailed on her own recognizance and I spoke to her on the phone, telling her I would see the police.

The next morning I stopped thinking about it and went up to the Yard to see the drug squad. They had a thick folder full of scripts and other evidence. All I wanted to do—like Gerry on a previous occasion—was to get it over with, no solicitor, just cop a guilty plea. I was charged with possession of ten grains of heroin, obtained illegally from Doctor Ritchie, and bailed out for the night, my stepfather showing up to stand surety.

In the morning, with a guilty plea, there could be only one result: two weeks remand for reports, the usual form for addicts. The police tried to recommend bail—the police, as always, were fair with me—but the Man didn't want to know. Julia's case was thrown out of court.

Curtis's death—the latest in the line—had attracted some pressure and the authorities were in the process of modifying their methods. In cases of severe need, methadone, a weaker synthetic opiate, could be given orally. But the wheels of prison bureaucracy move slowly, and the routines hadn't been systematized.

Junkies went into the hospital wing, in common with arsonists, killers, homosexuals and spies, an interesting social barometer. The hospital was simply like a nuthouse with security cells downstairs and wards on top, unusual wards with the curious rule that nobody was allowed on their beds during the day.

After the interminable admission procedure with its medical examination, record-taking and clothes issue—from four in the afternoon until eleven at night—I was sent to a ward. But the prison industry was booming and, like Cane Hill, didn't have a bed for me. I was given a mattress to place on the floor, the screw came round telling his dirty stories and switching off the lights, and I got sick.

It was hard and horrible but nothing new any more. Somehow neither the doctor nor the methadone got to me. I stuck it for three days and then flaked out, waking up in a cell to myself and a prison officer with a glass of methadone. Pain and delirium and fear . . . Who was I? and how long . . . Listening to the guard dogs barking in the night . . . the first aircraft of the day as it passed overhead, at five every morning . . . No way out . . . No-one to blame.

After eight or nine days the prison psychiatrist saw me and told me that they weren't going to cut the methadone down any more, on the basis of needless suffering and the fact that I was due to go into hospital afterwards. He was going to recommend a conditional discharge. By then I was receiving enough of the stuff to hold me together, equivalent perhaps to half a grain of heroin.

I was able to get out of bed and they transferred me to a normal prison wing, which I loathed, chiefly because of the squalor and the food. Anyway the psychopaths were better company than the petty criminals in the wing.

There were difficulties with the reports; and I found myself doing almost a month's remand instead of the original fortnight, with trips to court to break the monotony. Back after the second remand I went through the admission procedure all over again. But this time I wasn't so sick and was learning a few of the ropes, and I was determined to try and avoid the filthy B Wing. Every prisoner was accompanied by a white card on which was detailed his location, sentence and date of release or court appearance. In the indescribable confusion of admission it wasn't very difficult to steal one's card out of the pile for a minute. I borrowed a pen, found the space corresponding with my previous medical and inserted an initialled 'Send to hospital wing. Not to be transferred before release.'

Fortunately it was a young doctor who hadn't seen me before. He checked me over, read the card, signed underneath my comment and turned to my unfavourite screw: 'This man's for the hospital, Bennett.'

So at least I could get food brought in and have a bath. While the withdrawal never went away it wasn't unbearable; without sickness prison was easy to take. I spent the time trying to twist the red tape in my favour and reading Proust, given to me by the old lady in the hospital library. Proust is good prison reading. Life inside was far more secure and unthreatening than the junk scene without, death and destruction responding to rules with only the occasional sinister shadow . . . Screaming from the padded cell some nights, the occasional sadistic screw . . .

Relations with the other prisoners were superficial but easy. Talk of crime, though, bored me, and many prisoners spoke of little else. Harry Roberts, the police killer, was an exception; all he talked about was guns.

Flashes: the sheer physical abnormality of so many prisoners, grinning epileptics, pinched and shrunken old men, freaks with stumpy legs . . . In there for stealing bottles of milk and similar offences. It was like a sweeping ground, you never saw these people outside. Sad and depressing, because so many people were on remand for serious things; their cheerfulness was going to take a bang when they copped their seven years. The screws—old and amiable or young and sinister; the young ones bent their caps the way the Nazis did. . . .

In December I finally came up for sentence. Guest, the braying stipendiary, didn't like junkies and with a hard-nosed realism rejected the pressure from the liberals for a conditional discharge, giving me probation and six months condition of residence in Cane Hill. I knew that the doctors could sign me out of that anytime; even so I was a pretty shaken figure in court, unsure of the future, still very weakened by the withdrawal, trying to get my hands on the heroin that the prison authorities returned.

9

I arrived at Cane Hill in December 1966, initially rather oppressed at being the subject of a court order, still slightly ill. I was placed on a short reducing course of heroin for a week and then transferred back to methadone, the idea being to taper off the junk lust rather than letting it build up after forcible deprivation.

The hospital itself was huge and Victorian, rambling over the hilltop which gave it its name. Salter Ward, the drug unit, had been redesigned and didn't have the same claustrophobic atmosphere as the other wards; each of us had his own room, all of them opening on to a large, airy gallery with views over the grounds to the North Downs in the distance. Thin patches of snow were scattered over the hillside and in the crisp winter mornings I sat by the gallery windows watching our favourite patient, a distant, placid West Indian, taking salute and reviewing his troops from the summer house outside.

There were about ten of us. The emphasis was very much on living as a group, both in the sense of combining for group therapy and in terms of running the unit together. To a large extent each patient could decide his own course of treatment—as long as he could justify it to the staff and the rest of the group. There was no compulsion, the understanding being that everyone had come of his own free will—as I had originally—and shared the common goal.

In outline one tapered off drugs in stages and then proceeded to a more active involvement, firstly with the other patients and after that with the outside world. Methadone was used as a 'bridging' drug—it relieved the worst physical problems of withdrawal without providing any of the positive rewards and pleasures of smack. In theory, therefore, one came off methadone only after enough of an interval had elapsed to separate one from the old heroin routine, the possibility being offered that physical trauma and 'mental' need could be dealt with at different stages.

In parallel with the medical side of treatment we operated a system of limited freedom; during the early stages of withdrawal, when junk desire was strongest, we were confined to the unit. As junk need diminished so more licence was given, firstly to go into the hospital grounds, then to the local town, finally home on weekend leave.

I was soon content enough. Julia was able to visit as often as she liked. We enjoyed a powerful strengthening of our scene after the stresses of the previous months, long bouts of lovemaking in the privacy of my room, sampling the delicacies that she brought down from Fortnum's—the hospital food was atrocious and disgusting, acknowledged as such by all the staff—and generally relaxing. Angie had returned from the cave she inhabited in Positano to make a film in London. She got to know one of the other patients and the four of us were able to enjoy the illusion—or perhaps the reality—that we were on a health farm, spending whole days together, temporarily untouched by the presence of junk.

There was, however, the purpose of being in there; and that wouldn't just go away. Being the subject of a court order, I now had a complete inner cop-out to reinforce my original reservations; but a part of me wanted very much to be able to come off.

There were some hard realities straight away. The theory of the 'bridging' drug didn't work very well in practice and some of us were getting mildly dependent on the methadone injections, resisting the idea of quick cessation. The consultant in charge, who was the best doctor I ever met in the junk field, was aware of the problem but hadn't found a way round it. Every effort was made to get people completely off as quickly as possible; but it wasn't easy.

On the other hand nothing else worked very well either, fast withdrawal, slow withdrawal, bridging drugs, aversion therapy or surgical intervention. Within the framework of general ignorance the Salter Ward offered any addict the opportunity and tools to find his way off if he wanted to. And some succeeded.

The other patients were a mixture from the range of addict society. There were a few like David, a simple lad, placid and bovine, an ideal patient who never got very sick or upset: all the doctors had to do was point him in the right direction and he would be all right. Until he got outside and someone pointed him back again. But addicts like David were rare, though gradually becoming more frequent as more people got hung up under the influence of a group. Most of them were fiercely unwilling to be influenced by anyone at all; and this was perhaps the only common denominator amongst us, coming as we did from different age groups and social backgrounds.

The two I got to know best at first were Phillip and Mike. Phillip was a Sanskrit student and general head who'd lost his way. He was a little younger than me and hadn't been hooked for very long, a forceful but friendly man with an openness that was uncommon amongst users. But he'd been hung up on methedrine as well as smack and had developed a bad case of the bugs.

Under late-withdrawal stress he felt that insects and small creatures pursued him and lodged under his skin. Once he called me in to look in a mirror with him and observe something walking across his eyeball. I couldn't see anything but it was useless to argue. After he had been off a little while he was all right—unless he cracked up, sneaked out up to town and scored, as most of us did at one time or another. It was futile for him to try and conceal the fact. We always knew when he been out because he started picking his face to pieces and looking guilty and withdrawn.

When he was like that the only way he believed he could get rid of the creatures was to burn them; and he was always getting hounded by the rest of us—'Phil's at it again'—after we found piles of smouldering paper all over the unit. Unfortunately for him the hospital kitchens—one in each ward—were infested with cockroaches and other bugs of considerable courage. Often I used to walk into the kitchen late at night to make a cup of coffee and find Phillip rigid and transfixed by a couple of cockroaches circling around him, traces of blackened paper at his feet. But he was a lovely guy.

Mike was the chap making time with Angie. I had met him a few times outside and I got on with him because he was one of the more hip of the inmates and easily the speediest. But he was an all-time hustler who wound himself into greater and greater complications, a manipulator on a grand scale. He was the same age as me and had been using about the same length of time, graduating to junk from a career as a beat-cum-hustler. Dark-haired and heavy-featured, he apparently had traces of gypsy blood but his antecedents were impossible really to pin down: the only hard evidence of his past was a thin file in his room containing press cuttings of the wealthy young women he had seduced. Mike could be seen in some of them, leering at the camera from a dark coffee cellar on the South Coast under the headlines like: 'King of the Beatniks and the Girl who Loves him.'

But Mike wasn't ready to come off, and his attempts to evade the issue led him into a maze of difficulties. After a short but dynamic stay of a couple of months, during which he somehow obtained more smack than he had done outside, collaborated with me in obtaining hallucinogens from one of the hospital doctors, and amassed a dosage card for sleepers, tranquillizers and assorted uppers which resembled a catalogue, the other patients finally got insecure and asked him to leave. His last few weeks were a balancing act as he hypnotized and dominated the others into believing that he was making progress and should be left alone.

'But Mike,' said one of the braver sprits, 'you're always stoned, all the time. How can you call it a cure?'

But Mike's mad hustling was largely a reaction to the stress of coming off. We all suffered from it in one form or another. Some of us grew moody, as I did; others got depressed or hysterical. The ones who wound themselves up into a speedy hysteria rarely stayed for long. The most awkward reaction, and one that baffled us all in our attempts to help, was that of Danny, a young Glaswegian. I had met him at my second doctor's surgery, a thin and wiry guy in a Nureyev cap, full of energy.

Danny entered the unit just before I did and took to his bed. There he stayed, rising in the early stages for the occasional meeting, later only moving any part of himself for the most pressing reasons. He was still in bed when I left after seven months, grown flaccid and puffy. Danny became the scandal of the ward, our dark secret shut in a room that more and more resembled a vault, a subject for attacks from hospital administrators who had heard rumours about him and who, as is their way, valued tidiness and 'responsiveness' above all.

'But what actually is the matter with him?' asked one of the senior male nurses of a group of us once.

'Well it's like this, Mr James,' answered Phil. 'His father came down and threw an apple into his back . . .' But the reference to Kafka went unnoticed. In the other wards Danny wouldn't have got much food and might even have received an exploratory thick ear; in Salter Ward he was protected, a standing grievance to the hospital executives who didn't like the idea of an experimental unit much anyway.

This was a real problem: the gulf between normal hospital operating methods and the drug unit routine was almost too great to bridge. Nursing staff had to work in a completely new fashion for which their training hadn't prepared them and moreover were actually accountable to the patients for their behaviour. The younger nurses often found it an adventure; the senior staff—and every ward had to have a senior nurse—found it much more difficult. Many charge nurses had begun their training in the days before chemotherapy, when violent patients had to be dealt with 'firmly', and had found it difficult to relate to the new regime in the early fifties. To deal with self-governing junkies they had to alter the patterns of a life-time and unsurprisingly most of them didn't want to.

And we weren't our own best public relations men. There was a casual, scruffy and anarchic atmosphere in the ward which was always likely to grate on nurses, accustomed as they were to the formal rules and discipline which can keep death and suffering at bay, an illusion of control. Under the stress of sickness and the post-withdrawal blues few of us presented a very admirable sight.

One of us, for example, got rid of his tensions by retreating into a room on his own and methodically breaking windows, never admitting that it was he who had done so. This irritated all of us, so much so that we were driven to violence to stop him. If we reacted like that what did the nurses feel? And in the enclosed atmosphere with tension never far beneath the surface it was easy to fall into the game of trying to get whatever one could out of the nurses. Mike wasn't the only one; what might start as an attempt to get an extra sleeping pill out of a nurse for the hell of it and to kill the boredom could easily degenerate into a wound-up and desperate bid for junk, the patient employing all of his battery of formidable techniques to bend things his way. Tiny incidents could turn into grievances, the whole thing snowballing into a painful confrontation in front of the others. It was so easy to lose a sense of proportion in the partial vacuum in which we all lived.

Those nurses who didn't crack up at the beginning were usually marvellous, even though we took them too much for granted. I remember there was a little Irishman whom, if I had the blues, I would hustle unmercifully to try and get the dangerous drug cupboard open. In my early days there I saw him as someone to take advantage of. One night I heard he was working in the ward opposite, a geriatric unit, and I went in to say hello. The sight of that little fellow moving smoothly and efficiently, surrounded by dying madmen in a Goyaesque vision of Hell, filled me with shame and self-disgust. All for twenty quid a week. But still, the next time I felt that junk-need. . . .

There was always junk. The nurses could never be certain which side we were on. In the group meetings we would all sit there discussing our motivation and aspirations in the most sincere and genuine way, exchanging insights with the staff and other patients, attesting our dislike and fear of stuff. But later on someone might get the yen, the junk desire, and it all went out of the window for a moment.

Once a staff nurse walked through the gallery and into the adjacent office with thirty ampoules of methadone under his arm. He emerged a moment later and left the ward, clearly not having had time to lock the amps in the cupboard. (Cupboard? That gave you an idea of our potential—it was a wall safe.) With no other nurses about, the only other patient besides myself to witness the scene, a hulking psychopath named Lenny who'd done a bit of burglary, moved like lightning to grab a kitchen knife. In thirty seconds he had jemmied the door and was away into the grounds with the packets, with me just behind him.

We sat under a tree in the grounds, turning on. It was possible to get a buzz from methadone if you used a large amount.

'This is fucking mad, Lenny' I said, as I emptied the sixth

ampoule. 'Do you realize we're in here trying to get off?' We were, but there was a split. . . . Junk desire didn't go away, and the longer you were off the stronger the buzz.

Answers were hard to come by. Probably we all felt that simply being in hospital and withdrawing under medical supervision would help us get off without doing very much. Then we came off and usually found that we still wanted to take junk—and no-one knew what to do about it. I was the most cynical and perhaps the least optimistic of the patients, but even I was a little shaken by the sensation of having strayed into an area where nobody knew what to do—like a new disease, looking up and seeing lack of confidence in a doctor's eyes for the first time.

At that time there were still so many things I didn't know. Most important perhaps was the fact that 'treatment' and 'cure' were medical metaphors for a problem that couldn't be approached medically. It took me a long time to learn that a 'cure' in the sense of intervention from outside, either technical or human, was an impossibility, did not, in fact, exist. Like some of the others I tried to take consolation in my ignorance; I was in hospital, therefore I was getting 'well'.

Group therapy, behaviourist psychology, neo-Freudian insight therapy, encounter groups . . . Reading Freud, Jung . . . Something unconvincing and conceptual about Freud's descriptions of the unconscious, his biography—I noted with delight that he more or less initiated cocaine addiction . . . Wilhelm Reich . . . Long debates about Gurdjieff and Ouspensky . . . did they help? R. D. Laing, Michel Foucault, B. F. Skinner . . . Much literature fell into two classes, either we couldn't relate it to junk or else it tended to be rubbish: a theory a day keeps real thought away, all these mad doctors with their 'theories' on drug addiction . . . Take your choice.

We went through our therapy and interaction, prepared for a difficult ride through the territory of the unconscious leading to a cessation of 'symptoms'; instead we found ourselves wrestling with the most insane problems; every angle of approach to junk brought one up against the questions: Who were we? What part of us was it that wanted junk? Which was the 'real' us? Did we have free will? Just why did we want to live without junk? Was one part of us 'unhealthy' and bound for destruction? And if so, how could we separate that part?

The problem of will. Not will-power but the roots of one's will, where it began and ended. Aspiration indicated one course of action, junk desire another. Which was the true will? In the beginning was desire. Why resist the desire? Because one wanted to live without junk. But, manifestly, 'wanting to live without junk' had little meaning; it was words and hope. What one *wanted* was visible, surely, in one's actions, not words; and our actions and the roots of action tended to point towards using junk again. There were no maps of the will.

Many of the patients worked hard on the basis that their addiction was unconsciously motivated. But translating insight into action was something else. Those doctors who had faith in orthodox analytic techniques with junkies were unable to explain how junk desire was attenuated in practice. Presumably it was just meant to go away when inner conflicts had been resolved. But whether Freudian therapy related to anything real, or whether it depended on the gradual acceptance of an alternative framework of existence validated by an outsider, didn't matter; all too often it failed to give any results. Once someone had used stuff, theoretical unconscious motivation became increasingly irrelevant to the problems of junk desire or need; for that need came from within, not from the mind alone but from the cells as well, as valid and undeniable as the sex drive.

Whatever the words, whatever models of need were constructed, that integrated desire for stuff was present, apparently a part of the metabolism. Junk was its own definition of truth or reality, beyond words or logic. Just as any real junky laughed at the idea of placebo treatment, aware that once smack was in your veins you *knew* it beyond question of doubt or thought, so you *knew* junk desire and junk relief in a sense that was beyond theories. And it was left to you to cope with, ultimately on your own.

The possibility raised its head that for a number of people addiction was an unfortunate, specific condition that couldn't be relieved, to use the weary language of medicine again. A junky could be considered as a blind alley mutant, unfortunate enough to have discovered a technique for direct consciousness control. In effect the junky had a tap in his arm, plumbed into a chemical modification system. Such a technique, perversely, was in some ways the realization of a human dream.

And how many people were going to be able to resist that tap in their body? Every addict in the hospital, after all, had been brought up to believe in altering things by science and medicine—the old hopeful ideas: science will soon be able to . . .; we can *eradicate* mental illness; sickness can be *conquered* with drugs; starvation, obesity, angst and baldness, anxiety, poverty and premature ejaculation can all be *removed* if the intervention is correct. So was it that 'unnatural' to use a tap on your consciousness? More unnatural than an electrode in your brain, a transplant in your chest? That aspect of the junky was a nodding caricature of all of us.

And surrounding us in our little ward were two thousand mental patients being stuffed full of largactil, phenthiazine, librium, valium, chloral hydrate, mandrax, tofranil, ritalin, carbrital, phenergan and aventyl; drooping, gawking and sagging from the shit they were filled with, many of them to remain on the drugs for the rest of their lives, working their way back to 'normality'.

In the spring I went on weekend leave for the first time. Walking down the hill to the railway station I felt that I might be accomplishing something, at least in the sense that I no longer had my crushing habit. But I was still getting three injections of methadone daily to be maintained until I could do without any chemical support. I was pretty sure by then, however, that my stay in hospital was going to end inconclusively.

After all the words, spirals and marathons of interpretation, eventually it came down to the question: what else did I want? Ultimately debates on motivation were inconclusive one way or the other; the question 'could one have stopped using if . . .?' was meaningless. To know that I could have given up using junk when I wanted to would have been a relief: but as for taking the steps away from it in practice, I couldn't or wouldn't do it.

Cane Hill could only be a rest and refuge. I was still far from understanding the forces, old or new, that drove me, and I began to think that one couldn't understand the junk forces without knowing the roots of one's whole behaviour, for the two were intertwined. And who ever reached that level of knowledge? I wondered if it would come, if it ever came, from intercourse with drugs rather than flight from them. Sure, all of us in the unit wanted freedom from smack or, something slightly different, mastery over it. But mastery was not to be gained (one cannot master bullets, only learn to aim the gun); and the desire for freedom was a fragile one, based as it was more on the negative aspects, fear and breakdown, than on positive growth from inside.

However necessary it might seem in terms of personal survival, one could not just invent new goals. My life, any individual's life, came from within; any situation was the end-product of a continuous line of events and a reflection of the total make-up. To stop using junk implied a concern for the future, a balanced regard for one's life, a certain attitude towards integration which by the nature of things just was not there. They couldn't be conjured up; we are what we are.

One couldn't discuss junk in isolation, in terms of the Ego alone. To make such a radical change meant opting for something else, an accommodation with society and its mores—especially in the context of a hospital cure, dictated by exigencies rather than true will. For without a growth away from junk, without a real knowledge of one's own possibilities, one was thrown back on accepting or rejecting the views of others, of society, as relayed by professionals. And my attitude to society was not positive.

I had no particular contempt for society and 'straight' people, unlike some junkies, and not the slightest wish that others should behave as I did. Equally their goals, patterns and daily existence left me coldly unmoved. I had only one life here in this body, I felt, and perhaps the mistakes and failings had to be mine, unguided by others.

Not even guided by the example and warnings of a cultural background and the human store of common sense and caution—for that storage house had manifestly lost touch with its roots and truths. Perhaps a cure in an institution might work if society's representatives inside could offer knowledge on how to live as human beings on this earth. Looking around, I believed that we had lost that knowledge and were fast losing even the conviction.

But at least the patients could offer some strength to one another; the experience of living in a close-knit group with common goals offered us the chance to grow. Wayward individualists all of us, we were willing to compromise and try to work together in a way that was impossible for us in the larger group outside. Here one could see the immediate consequences of one's actions and understand how the whole was guardian for each part.

Julia and I stayed together at weekends from my first period of leave until I came out of hospital for good. But I had developed no real aims, no plans to take a job. We marked time in a comfortable fashion although it quickly filtered through to Julia that hospital had accomplished no miracles, that I was still hung up.

When I first went on leave, 1967 had arrived and the drug culture had finally surfaced without my knowing it.

Three months or so. It was like coming out of prison after years.

'Why are all these idiots wearing beads?' I asked testily of Julia the first time we walked along the Kings Road together, unaware of the way drugs, smoke, and acid particularly, had become a fashionable, visible cult. 'Where the fuck are they at?'

Old acquaintances, semi-straight people who'd been frightened of my whole scene—now I met them in town, growing their hair and asking if I wanted a snort, man.

Michael's boutique off the Kings Road, shadowy art nouveau interior, the basement a representation of the unconscious, Mike striding and bending in prismatic shades, full of acid and methedrine, preaching liberation . . . The UFO club, acid rock music, air of happy chaos, a night club that sold apples and bananas for the trippers instead of alcohol . . . The Eastern invasion, people looking for guides to consciousness, no longer any to be found in the West. . .

Nice to be borne along for a while . . . Heads versus straights, the heads were in the ascendent . . . Intense friends calling round to announce the Revolution in consciousness; too big to stop now, they told me, the Age of Aquarius was arriving; society would be sapped from within . . . Lots of hope about that summer. . .

Fun that it was, there was something idle and shallow about the whole business. Sandy's ideas on the big scale, mosaic of undifferentiated mysticism, rock music pseudo-philosophy, stoned fashions and hipster argot—it was all delightful if you were just having a good time. But a better world? Surely nothing worthwhile could be accomplished that easily; all the real questions were being begged . . . Ill-defined and badly expressed hopes that if everyone could develop a turned-on outlook then they wouldn't want to fight or exploit any more; people would give each other flowers. . .

They made Herbert Marcuse sound like a realist. I remember him at a symposium on liberation that summer, opening his speech: 'I am very happy to see so many flowers here and that is why I want to remind you that flowers, by themselves, have no power whatsoever. . .'

And the dark side soon began to show, the hard hustlers moving in to exploit the scene, cannabis plants printed on carrier bags, music promoters, rubbishy cheap goods with a 'head' angle. Was there any tinsel that my generation wouldn't buy? Instant gurus—we were looking for leaders again, always leaders. And the dark, homegrown version—-people soon found out that if you gave someone their first trip and talked them through it the right way, then they woke up to worship you, roll at your feet, plead to fuck you. Charlie Manson was on his way.

The Nuthouse seemed like a repository of sanity. There, away from the tinsel kings like Richard Neville and poor John Lennon—they wanted to teach us!—there at least some work was being done, some attempt was being made to live with others as freaky as you, some attempts at running a community, however odd the community was . . . not just hopes and spokesmen.

Interesting juxtaposition that spring and summer—the belief in anarchic communities that was so prevalent outside and the bid within to make it work, even if it was on a protected basis. But outside people could apparently believe that the question of human dominance would just go away, and with it the complications and the need for rules. Inside we recapitulated the old problems, applicable to all, addicts or non-addicts: How did you take decisions fairly, how could you stop the stronger personalities in any group from getting their way at the expense of the weaker just by force of will? What did you do about the gulf between addicts like myself, and the others who had some family or private means, and the people who got a pound a week from the hospital? What sanctions could we justify for destructive behaviour, near-anarchists ourselves with a reluctance to participate in punishing anyone? There were no easy answers.

Terry the jazz musician 'graduated' from our group, cured but reluctant ever to play again, for fear of the music environment. Placid Dave left quietly, also cured in the clinical sense, but with none of the real problems completely solved. Mike had also left—and in despair had attempted to kill himself soon afterwards. How much was that our fault for having excluded him?

Phillip was making progress, the blackened paper and facial ravages hardly seen any more. His new peace of mind was reflected in the music he played on a Moroccan pipe, the notes floating from his room in the middle of the night, tailing away as he walked out into the grounds on his own, playing to the summer darkness.

Two or three departures out of our dozen, their places being taken by new people. Austin was the most interesting of these, undercover member of straight society, a junky working for the Health Service as an auditor. At the initial interview I thought he looked the model of an administrator, a respectable suit and sober tie, briefcase and short hair—but he wore no socks.

Austin was about my own age with a Ladbroke Grove and Tangier background before taking a job. His background before that was something of a mystery that he didn't enlarge on, except that he wrote books and had been using junk for years. Junk quietened something inside him, something possibly rather frightening, for as he came off and began to relate to other people more he emerged as one of the most formidable men that I'd ever met with an extraordinary sense of potential violence about him. We liked each other but in such claustrophobic surroundings and given the nature of our respective personalities—from a certain distance.

Danny still slept. . .

None of us knew what to do about Danny. If he wanted to stay in bed, then as far as the unit was concerned he had an absolute right to do so; and in the junk context coercion would probably have masked the problem. After some months it was clear that he would be as well off in a bed at home as he was in the unit; but no-one wanted to ask him to leave in case it sent him back to junk. We waited.

And I stumbled along, my methadone rising to five ampoules a day until I was withdrawn once again, this time to nothing. Feeling naked again, I started going up to town and scoring once or twice a week, unsettling the others who found out about it. I couldn't go much further in hospital.

But the unit itself had its troubles. On top of all the old problems of staffing and the controversies over methods of treatment, there was a more serious difficulty. A new head of nursing had been appointed—in mental hospitals nurses have more real power than doctors—and unlike his predecessor he was unsympathetic to the unit. There was a reliable rumour that its days were numbered. The staff situation got worse; and the mainstay of the ward, the only charge nurse who truly understood the place, was transferred, told he had been 'indoctrinated' by the junkies.

The new regime was obtrusive, not so much by clearly misguided initiatives such as this one, but more by an impression of being on the watch for irregularities. The old chief, a bluff and decent man of retirement age who'd brought us whisky and cigars at Christmas and accepted a couple of drags from a spliff in return, had been content to ignore the grosser failings amongst us, partly at least because it was believed that the unit might bring fame to the hospital if it was a success. The new team were more cynical and perhaps more realistic. But once people started looking for faults in that unit, they'd be overwhelmed, for almost everything that went on in there was an affront to conventional concepts of treatment and administration; the place could never be justified from a defensive position. If they needed more ammunition they were sure to get it, though perhaps not in the sense that they expected.

It was James who passed the rumour on to me. I'd been friendly with him since entering and he was the best informed, having been there the longest. A tall young guy, languid and good-looking, a refined bisexual from a country family, he had spent nearly a year in the unit and was now caught in a vacuum between junk life and going out clean, unable to make the transition. He dealt with the problem by going to sleep; under stressful circumstances he was incapable of staying awake. For the record he was classified as a narcoleptic; but clinical diagnosis in that context had very little meaning. A nurse woke him in the morning by placing a dexedrine tablet on his tongue.

Those old post-withdrawal blues. . . .

On the other hand I had founded, without joining, the corn-flakes club for those whose PW blues took a contrasting form. Certain patients, those whose nakedness after junk showed in insecurity with others, used to get hold of sleeping pills in some quantity. Before bedtime they dropped them, the period before unconsciousness a deep bath of relaxation with others as they wandered round gabbling to all the people whom they were unable to relate to sober—talking faster, more intimately and incoherently all the time.

Billy was the fourth member of the club (I was an expert because for some reason I attracted them) and the most prominent—a cheerful, thickset cockney from Fulham whose tough exterior concealed deep inner fears about his own strength and masculinity. After a while you knew when it was coming: Billy would wend his way to the kitchen, make a disorganized bowl of cereal—or worse, creamed rice—and stagger from room to room, chatting and reaching vacantly for the spoon until the end came. A sudden jerk of the neck and splat! in went the face, slap into the creamy bowl. Like a ritual. Carry him off to bed.

Billy disliked being on his own and at his request shared the small, long-stay dormitory with James. As one might imagine, the relationship did not prosper: club members irritated James intensely and, unlike the rest of us, he had no room to flee to. But he did have a sharp line in put-downs and mercilessly deflated Billy whenever he got too boring, judging to a nicety how far he could go without copping a hiding.

At a group meeting one day Billy, who definitely lacked judgement, told us how he had bought some shotguns and wanted to do some shooting in the grounds. A shotgun in a nuthouse? Staff and patients gently pointed out the difficulties and the idea was forgotten.

But not by Billy. After his first weekend leave the word went round that he had returned with a suspiciously long parcel. Incredible as it sounds, none of us did anything about it, satisfied when Billy told us that he had brought no ammunition and would keep the gun in his locker, unwilling to blow the whistle on him to the staff—who, needless to say, knew nothing—in case trouble arose.

It was clear to me that he had a thing about guns and

violence; but I never took him very seriously, thinking that the gun was stolen and he was hiding it, laughing when he got into one of his rages. Billy was by no means a figure-of-fun psychopath; some of the time he could be a shrewd realist, not at all stupid on the everyday level. But when he stuffed himself with sleepers. . . .

I underestimated those blues again. One night as a couple of us were having a mildly illicit joint in the lounge next to the dormitory . . . the crash of both barrels at two a.m. in a hospital ward was horrendous, like a bomb going off. We recovered, stared at each other, and ran into the dormitory, finding a mad parody of High Noon. Billy was swaying, eyes drooping and stoned, in his oversmall pyjamas, the shotgun waving under one arm, smoke still trickling out of the barrels. He handed me the gun without a struggle and I turned to James, beginning to laugh. James was standing, or rather crouching, at the foot of his bed, white-faced and frozen, rigid and open-mouthed. The whole bed was ripped and shattered by twelve-bore pellets and James's Nepalese bed-cover, of which he was inordinately fond, was destroyed.

There was no chance of hushing it up, the heavy mob were already on their way. A supervisor took possession of the gun and Billy was carried off to bed once more. He maintained, then and afterwards, that he had only wanted to give James a fright, stop his needling. But as James had been sitting on his bed when Billy took aim from six feet away. . . .

'He was aiming at me all right,' James told me in the safety of my room over a calming joint. 'But he was so stoned I had time to jump. Mad bastard.'

After which it is surprising to record that the unit survived for more than other year. An enquiry was held and Dale, the consultant in charge, had to agree to a formal meeting between the hospital administrators and the unit 'to discuss grievances and methods of treatment'. It was rotten luck for Dale; and we all felt we had let him down by doing nothing about Billy and the gun in the first place.

And I decided to leave, perhaps fearing that we might all be done away with one dark night if we continued in our present way. I had gone as far as I could anyway. Increasingly I felt that I couldn't do any more in a group, my scoring was simply a drag on the whole unit and my court order had expired. Regretfully I asked Dale if he would go on seeing me as an out-patient until I decided what I was going to do.

I was still there on the day of the meeting, the early part of which we spent in trying to get Danny out of bed to make a token appearance, to no avail. I hoped that none of the outsiders would try and speak to him, for he knew by now that he was the subject of controversy: any enquiries were likely to be met by a hail of Glaswegian abuse.

An air of reasonableness was maintained for much of the time at the meeting, an atmosphere that was quite manifestly artificial. The administrators were unwilling to say exactly what they wanted—the abolition of the unit in its present form—and contented themselves with attacking 'abuses', their concern for the inmates being stressed continuously. But one only had to list the abuses to see that without them nothing would be left of the unit.

I took little part in the dialogue, disheartened at the scene, and anyway able to see the other point of view. It had always seemed a miracle to me that the place functioned at all within the Health Service; and as it was in opposition to almost every orthodox tenet of treatment, it was hardly to be expected that administrators with sincerely opposed views would protect it. It was no use getting hung up on 'patient power'— patients had no power and never could have except for the power of their purse. An old story. Such units, I thought, would probably function very well in a private context, depending as they did on indulgence. Indulgence could always be bought, but was less easily given.

In the face of my cynical lack of interest it was left to Austin to talk in terms of right and wrong—never my strong suit in debate. He was not only a powerful person, but was also extremely articulate and perceptive. Warming to his theme he recapitulated the arguments of the new chief and pointed out the latent hostility that his smooth words concealed, stressed the concern of the administration for 'management' rather than treatment, described the way in which the mental patients in the rest of the hospital were reduced to faceless robots under restraint, and questioned the normality of the staff themselves. He ended with a violent verbal attack on the chief nurse and his beliefs, a performance of impressive force that left the assembled executives red-faced and gaping as he strode out of the room. After which the meeting broke up in hushed disarray. The feelings of the administrators were easy to imagine—a Frankenstein's monster had been created which smuggled guns into the wards and attacked them like savages in public.

I left shortly afterwards, grateful for what the unit had offered me, but lacking immediate and obvious gains. Of the others, Danny eventually transferred to a Scottish hospital, James and Phillip stayed, but couldn't completely free themselves at that time. Both Austin and Billy came to violent ends, sadly but unsurprisingly. Poor Billy hanged himself in prison a couple of years later, and Austin, that terrible temper of his dogging him to the end, was knifed to death in a fight—reminders that, underneath all the absurdities and excesses, none of us had been in there for fun.

10

Over the next few months I hung suspended, neither getting a real habit again nor doing anything concrete to avoid it happening. Prison, hospital and the concentration on the idea of getting cured had generated their own dynamic so that, irrespective of what I wanted, it seemed utterly wasteful to revert to my addiction.

But the will was not there. Left to myself I would have got hooked again pretty quickly. But there was Julia to consider, as well as parents and relatives who believed I was more or less cured. A half-hearted sense of obligation—half-hearted because I knew it wasn't enough—dictated many of my actions; and this vacuum at the centre of things accounted for the pattern of our life as I consistently evaded the issue, the strong front which I had always maintained, or which others had found for themselves, crumbling in the face of realities.

I had seen other addicts in a similar position and had watched them crack under the tension, like Moss, more stretched and pressurized than they had been when fixing all the time. Re-addiction, when it came—and it was survived—often provided a welcome sense of relief.

Julia had her own life to lead, after all. I could hardly expect her to go on waiting for me to get off stuff for ever. My own feelings that I was bound to disappoint all her hopes in the end became self-fulfilling as I retreated even more into myself. And coupled with this pessimism, there was the awful sensation of feeling like an invalid all the time, a sense of helplessness and inadequacy in the face of events which had never been there when I had been hooked. Being hooked had its own take-it-or-leave-it validity, one was doing something at least. Caught half-way, trying to do things I didn't really want to do, lacking all conviction, I felt like a trapped mouse. No relationship could last long under these circumstances.

In an effort to run away, we decided to go abroad for the winter, hoping optimistically that a change of scene might alter the situation. Relatives helped with some money and Julia continued to work. We saved while I oscillated.

I continued to see Dale for a time, getting a small, supportive script for methadone. Methadone itself had turned out to be another illusion, another uneasy half-way house, providing a spurious belief that one was accomplishing something by not using heroin; it was just as physically addictive as smack in the long run. Increasingly I augmented or replaced it with heroin.

The government had announced their intention of replacing GP treatment with designated drug treatment centres in 1968. As the time drew closer, so it was easier to find doctors who were willing to prescribe for slightly dubious reasons. Trying to save, not wanting to spend fortunes in the West End again, I sought them out.

Doctor Imrie was the first, his name given to me by one of the patients in Cane Hill. One afternoon, a month or two after leaving hospital, I went to see him. His surgery was in the middle of Soho, at the top of four flights of narrow and creaking stairs. And his waiting room, when I eventually reached it, was something straight out of Dickens—a tiny, fusty alcove redolent of nineteenth-century clerks. Doctor Imrie appeared at his surgery door after a few moments, apparently having been waiting for a patient—any patient—to show.

The good doctor must have been over eighty years old and looked like a friend of Burke and Hare, snow-white locks falling onto a winged collar, pince-nez perched at the end of his squirrel nose. Inside, the surgery was equally unusual, nothing in it seemingly any younger than the doctor himself. Curious and primitive medical instruments hung on the walls in their original wooden and glass cases; his stethoscope was an early model, tinged with verdigris, and on his desk stood an upright telephone.

I stated, gently, that my problem was not actually a physical one, in short that I wanted—

'Enough, enough,' bleated the old man, placing a withered finger to his lips, 'I shall make my diagnosis and then indicate a course to be followed. In silence if you please.'

He touched his stethoscope to the side of my neck,

manipulated my shoulder blades and, apparently satisfied that he had fulfilled his oath, settled back into his chair.

'Young man, you are suffering from a serious and chronic condition and it is clearly my duty to assist.' He leaned forward. 'How much do you need?' After some desultory Scottish bargaining we arrived at a figure. Particulars were taken in a spidery hand and a script written out on tiny notepaper. I passed over his two-guinea fee which he made a pretence of dismissing as a detail.

'And remember now, my young man,' said the doctor as I headed for the rhomboid doorway, 'discretion, discretion. An important maxim in medical affairs.'

There was always the risk that Imrie might drop dead while writing the prescriptions ('that's all right,' said Phillip when I mentioned the possibility, 'just wave a new pound note under his nose') and in other ways, too, he lacked suitability.

Under the pressures of increasing numbers of hungry junkies, the doctor began to crack. After a little while the drug squad called on him with some friendly advice, leaving him in a state of paranoid terror. He took to hiding in the lurching garret; after he had been coaxed out, each interview began with a blank refusal to prescribe followed by an argument, resolved each time by the production of my wallet. But I tired of the scene and went to look for another doctor, finding the meetings pathetic and distasteful.

Doctor Knight had no fears of the police or anyone else and certainly discretion was not a word that ever crossed his lips. Nor could one complain about the age of his surgery, for he was the first practitioner I had met who didn't possess one.

He was an interesting, if unbalanced, personality who gave me my first consultation in the unlikely surroundings of the public lavatories in Piccadilly. But the practice was a roving one: in his battered doctor's bag he carried a headed notepad and a gold scorpion. These two items were set out wherever he could find a space and converted a pub table or café booth, a friend's bed or an upturned box, into a doctor's desk.

A tall, balding man of about sixty with piercing eyes, an ex-naval surgeon fallen on hard times, he prescribed as much junk as I wanted with no nonsense about treatment or cure.

Here was a relationship I understood and appreciated, refreshed by the absence of doubletalk. The knowledge, quickly acquired, that we were both Scorpios inclined him to treat me generously. Payment was once again on the nail: an alcoholic and a compulsive gambler, the doctor always had a pressing need for money.

Meeting him was difficult, however. The doctor had attracted a certain amount of attention from police and press, with the result that even when he found temporary premises he was likely to be evicted without notice. It was wise to seek him out well in advance of one's needs, allowing two days to track him down.

For a while he found a base in one of the expensive but non-U hotels in Bayswater—the kind with fountains in front of the desk. Bemused tourists observed the daily pack of hardened addicts spreading into the road, coughing and sneezing in the cold mornings, occasionally passing out in the doorway. I wondered what the doctor must be paying for his rooms. Ultimately not enough—for I arrived one day to a scene of panic: junkies clucking and searching agitatedly for the doctor, a large and tattered pile of belongings dumped on the pavement. He was taken in for a while by Joss, thereby acquiring a practice in Cheyne Walk, Joss at last achieving his ambition of getting more methedrine than he could use.

By now I was getting a definite heroin habit and we decided it was time to leave London. Patrick, Julia's brother, who taught art in Positano in the summer, arranged to rent us his villa for a few months; and with a few grains of smack, and some oral methadone to taper me off, we left for Italy at the end of November.

I was used to the early, physical part of withdrawal by now and the sickness wasn't unbearable, especially as I still wasn't using very much. I was able to drive south from Rome, boosting myself with the last few tablets of smack and looking forward to some sunshine to ease my aching bones.

Snow fell south of Rome that winter. We arrived in a violent thunderstorm, and for some weeks gales continued to howl in from the Mediterranean, shaking the windows and rattling round the badly heated rooms. An inauspicious start to an unproductive stay. I took to my bed, huddling under the blankets, thinking ruefully of the sticky warmth of a Brixton prison cell.

Once again I was off stuff, and once again bereft. After a few weeks I was reasonably fit, physically, but apathetic and uncommunicative, sitting miserably in the house, passive and unfriendly.

The others launched a programme to bring me round, each in their own way. Patrick brought back large quantities of alcohol—which my liver rejected—and inveigled the village pornographer into laying on film shows. Julia thought that a refined diet might be the answer and ensured that a bottle of champagne—which my liver could accommodate—was usually at my side. Angie and her new girlfriend appeared with a chunk of opium and a variety of uppers and downers from the shadier Sorrento doctors.

It was no good. Even when the warmer weather came and there was more to do, I remained depressed and anti-social. It didn't help either that the villa was small and that Patrick, who had intended to move to Portugal for the winter, had been prevented from doing so. He was rather older than me and could be marvellously kind and helpful. But at the same time he was as self-destructive as I was in a different way; his painting wasn't going well and he was having some temporary difficulties with alcohol. It was difficult for anyone to sympathize with my stubborn moroseness day after day.

And Julia and I slipped further and further apart; I grew more defensive and isolated as I realized once again that I couldn't live without stuff. Did the 'man underneath' whom Julia had waited for so long exist at all?

Bored but tense all the time, I found my only relief in taking the hired Fiat up into the hills on my own every day, driving at lunatic pace along the winding Via Amalfatina, judging the bends closer and closer each time, finding release in self-created danger. It was usually touch and go. After an hour or two of this I would return, sweating and exhausted but temporarily relaxed.

One morning the line I'd worked out failed, workmen having arrived to mend the road. I put the car into a long, hurling skid and went off at the base of the hairpin, scattering signs and navvies into the dust, finally coming to rest on a bank, the car half turned over. I pulled myself out and walked back to the workmen for help—but they'd seen me and my driving before and expressed their opinion by pelting me with garbage.

Things came to a head when I made an excuse to return to London. Patrick, who always ran short in the winter months, wanted to go back to sell some antiques he owned, and I seized on the opportunity, telling the others that I wanted to collect some money we were owed and that the trip might do me good. Julia and I wished each other a wary goodbye as I left; she had sensibly decided to stay with Angie, quite aware of the likely consequences of the journey, but knowing that there was nothing she could do any longer.

In London the first move I made was to find Doctor Knight. I located him in the bowels of Stratford. His surgery was now some derelict office premises, dark, cavernous and sinister. An anglepoise lamp picked out the corner of the building he was using and spotlighted the golden scorpion.

I congratulated him on his new base and stability. The doctor was immune to irony and he dismissed the question with a wave of his hand as though he were in Harley Street. Offering him a considerable sum of money, I asked for supplies for the next month, tired of messing about with small fixes. And I left with a sheaf of scripts cold in my hand, cashing them at different chemists to avoid the questions that such quantities from such a source might arouse.

Then I wended a crazy and irresponsible path back to Italy with Patrick, who was no stranger to dissipation even though he didn't use junk. Somehow the journey took three weeks instead of the few days originally allotted, as we got hung up time after time with different crowds in a stoned and aimless debauch. But it was rather funless, for me at least—anything to evade the issues. Even then, when the logic of my actions must have been visible to everyone but myself, I changed course and sold a lot of the stuff to a hard-eyed English emigré in Rome, returning to Positano after an absence of a month intending to take to my bed again.

But by then Julia was bombing out on the local amphetamine, confessing her utter despair with the turn things had taken, questioning how long we could go on any more, trying to make sense out of events that had slipped out of our grasp or control. For a few more days we dragged it out until a bitter and final row blew up, ending with Julia walking out into the night and then a fierce argument between Patrick and myself.

This was surely the end. Nothing lay ahead for us but pain, failure and more pain, probably until one of us killed ourselves. I sat alone, trying to reconcile the person I thought I was with the mayhem I was wreaking around me. Dawn came; Julia was still missing, Patrick had gone out. I packed a case, slipped out of the villa and caught the first train to Rome. After a few aimless days with a wayward contessa, attracted to the dope bottles rather than my body, I returned to London, the uncertainties of the past year at an end.

PART THREE

THE FAR SIDE

11

The sun was rising over the West End as I walked to the toilets to wash and have a morning fix. Soho, very early in the morning before the dust had risen, had a strange peacefulness about it, like a bathed and exhausted lover as the water vans cruised along, spraying the streets.

A sense of relief. All I wanted was junk. Visits to the doctor, prescriptions—and I had enough, nothing else mattered very much, neither people nor money, safety or comfort. I washed and shaved, talking to the other fellows waking themselves up beside me. My face stared out from the big mirror on the wall, tired but calm. I finished, gave the attendent a few pence with the towel I returned and walked off to get some breakfast.

1967 seemed like a bad dream in retrospect, a farrago of false hopes and expectations. Now I was facing the fact that the illusions were over, and accepting not just that I was an addict, but a very serious one. The way in which I had held myself together in the past, the impression of strength which I had given to others—and perhaps to myself—these things had masked a corrosive and shocking need to fix, as intense a need as any I had encountered. I had to acknowledge the fact, alternatives were out, the will was subverted from within.

I was meeting Julia later in the morning for the second time since we returned from Italy. I wondered what we could say to each other; the past was gone and so was 'the man underneath'. Never again would I live with a non-addict, not as long as I used stuff myself. And if the illusions of getting 'cured' were behind me, so was any more romancing with junk. There couldn't be any more making a style out of drugs, I reflected, no more parading myself, leading a double life, disguising the facts of drug addiction under a veneer and alibi of self-exploration. I had fooled myself and I had fooled Julia.

I met her in the Sands coffee house. When she first arrived, looking lovely but tired, more tired than I was, we talked brightly of unimportant things. Gradually we got into deeper waters. She was willing to start again. After three years, the latter part of which she had spent carrying me like a cross, she still hadn't written me off. A woman's love was something unbelievable. But was it love any more, I asked her, or was it now a mixture of other things, a reluctance to break with the past, habit, a sense of obligation and sympathy for me?

Things could never be the same, she told me.

Why was it so hard for me to say that I simply couldn't bear the responsibility of another, essentially innocent, person any more? I pointed out that the things she had said in Italy were true, true from beginning to end. There was no point in second thoughts now; as long as I was hooked we were just going to go on repeating the same patterns, only more seriously and more destructively each time.

She was unable to understand the change in me over the last month or two. And she asked me, with some perception, if I was somehow blaming her for the failure of my own hopes; she felt a hostility that had never been there before. Perhaps, subconsciously, I had done, always looking for someone else to blame, however guiltless they were. I didn't know, I had no faith at all in my own feelings towards others any more.

The words came out in a rush. I told her that drugs came first, before her, before everyone. That I was worthless to her, sickened by my own worthlessness and determined not to repeat our experience; that I couldn't live with anyone while pain and failure were so close; that I was disgusted with myself for having let her work and hope for so long. And I told her that I doubted if I ever could come off junk.

There was a silence. Had I been raising my voice? We returned to our food, both of us upset. There were so many other things to say; but it didn't seem to do any good. For the first time I was unsure of what she must be thinking. She brought the conversation back to a quieter level; we drank our coffee and left the restaurant. Outside I called a taxi for her, turned to say goodbye and held my hands out in a gesture of impotence. We didn't see each other again.

I went back to the streets. I had nowhere to live and no

money apart from the small amounts I could make selling a few pills. For a short time I had stayed with friends, moving on from one to another after a week or so. Afterwards I gravitated to the West End, preserving my anonymity, preferring not to see people who knew me.

I fell into the West End junky routine, sleeping with whoever I could find, staying with other junkies when I could, spending the nights in St James's Park or the public lavatories when there was nowhere else to go.

Of course there was an element of masochism in all this, an over-reaction to the difficulties I was in. Paradoxically there was also a hint of self-preservation—for I was close to the edge. The example of Moss and others was always at the back of my mind. So many had cracked after battling to give up stuff, drawn into a nexus from which there was little chance of escape, the realities of addiction replaced by a frantic and illusory campaign against the self until relapse was seen as the ultimate failure, suicide the only way out.

I was not, I told myself, going to die of self-respect. Complete acceptance was my own alternative and if it had a slightly hysterical and self-demeaning edge to it then at least it stopped me freaking and helped me find some sense of perspective. Nothing was forever. In time things would change and until then I could survive.

Full circle! After years of looking down my nose at the West End junkies I was now a member of the club myself, as sordid as the rest of them, selling stuff, scraping for food, keeping my eyes open for the main chance. The West End was becoming a harder scene than in the past, the old unorganized relationships breaking down as the new clinics took over from the doctors and began to squeeze supplies. Doctors were supposed to transfer their patients in the weeks before the April deadline; but drunken Doctor Knight had forgotten to refer half his patients and, along with many others, I had to schlep around from teaching hospital to teaching hospital trying to find a clinic to take me on.

I found a suitable unit on the last day, having had the chance to compare the bearable with the bad. My first encounter was with two weeping women who had also held out to the last moment and now found themselves cut adrift. Never having had a really supportive doctor and unworried at the prospect of small scripts needing black market additions—that would hardly be a new situation for me—I was undisturbed by the changeover.

For others it was different and I felt truly sorry for them, patients who had had close and secure relationships with their doctors for years, numerous older addicts like poor Anna Kavan who found themselves in limbo, at the mercies of inexperienced consultants and faced with the cold and rigid bureaucracy of any busy institution. My clinic was free of the grosser aberrations—mandatory group therapy, close supervision, compulsory reduction. But the future might be different, for the clinic was headed by a charmless fantasist who announced in public that within a year all his patients would be off heroin and placed on surrogates. Food for thought . . . but the fatuity of doctors no longer surprised me.

At my first interview I was confronted by an amiable Welshman who knew absolutely nothing about drugs or junkies. But I was unable to capitalize on his ignorance. We negotiated excitedly for half an hour, finally fixing a level of three grains a day and some ampoules of the worthless methadone. Impressed by his toughness and unable to work out why my onslaught for more was failing, I repeatedly asked him what exactly his criteria were for estimating my dosage. He prevaricated until it finally hit me towards the end of our interview:

'You're just dividing Doctor Knight's scripts by three, aren't you?'

He had the grace to laugh with me and admit it. It must have been as accurate as any of the other methods they used.

In order to get the supply at all I had to have a fixed address. My brother had a house in the suburbs and there I based myself, in one small room on the top floor. I rarely stayed there at first, using it as an alternative to the left luggage lockers in the West End, picking up my scripts from a chemist in Shaftesbury Avenue.

I kept my habit within reasonable limits, uninterested in taking massive amounts, and delaying as long as possible the day when my addiction might once more spiral out of control. I tried just once to get an extra script out of the clinic, but the experience was so exhausting that I didn't repeat the attempt and took my custom to the free market.

The first time I was offered Chinese smack I turned it down, aware of the dirt and impurities it contained, reluctant to start fixing anything less than pure heroin. But with English in short supply and increasingly expensive I managed to overcome my scruples. It was a brown, lumpy powder, sold in paper packets. Hong Kong immigrants had cornered the black market and the dealing and meetings took place in the Chinese quarter of Soho, in the doorways and alleys behind the fragrant restaurants, in the dusty betting shops and darkened billiard halls.

It had to be strongly heated but it usually cooked up clear with a strong opium smell; a different flash from the English variety, a fuzzy, slightly dirty sensation that came on slowly and hung around for hours, sending you on the nod.

A bit of a hustle to score, though. The Chinamen stayed off the Street as a rule and left the dealing ('running') in the hands of addicts, the worst type of addicts usually, brutalized by the gangsterish atmosphere and paranoia that surrounded the black market scene. Every time you copped there was likely to be trouble, with crooked runners, ersatz gear (yeastvite, make-up powder, brickdust) and increasing numbers of thugs, attracted by a scene where the victim could no longer go to the police.

At first I was as innocent as anyone, unaware of the changes that had taken place, copping my brickdust with the rest of them. But you had to harden up or stop scoring; for once it was known you were an easy target everyone tried to turn you over, the word got around. You simply had to be careful, making sure you didn't deal with strange runners unless they were introduced by someone, keeping your ears open to discover who had been doing what, honing the intuition that years of junk-taking had developed.

The first time anyone tried to rob me, the technique had a certain simplicity about it. A guy followed the runner and myself until we reached the alley in which the gear was stored. I had seen the fellow behind us; but I knew his face and, satisfied that he wasn't a policeman, I ignored him. We sorted out the deal and separated. I was walking through Covent Garden when I heard the footsteps running up behind me. In broad daylight the ruffian, Mad Phil—muscles but no brains, and certainly no finesse—took my arm and said:

'Right. Gimme the fucking packet or else.'

I looked around me; he was on his own. Well, if it had

been money I might have come across; but I was looking forward to that packet and wasn't giving it to anyone. So a mad brawl ensued; the guy eventually produced a knife and after some unpleasantness I got clear, my jacket in shreds, my neck slashed but the packet still snug in my shoe. It served me right for being so careless.

But incidents like that were pretty frequent if you spent any length of time on the Street. You learnt to cope with them or you stayed away. It was a far cry from the days when junk had seemed a gentleman's game.

And the amount of money required if one had a big Chinese habit was enormous, greater than I had ever spent in the past. It was turning into a New York scene. Some people got the bread by regular shoplifting or stealing from cars; others had to deal themselves; a few mugged for the money and yet others conned.

I was making it for a while with a girl who was hung up on large amounts, and she retained sufficient style and looks to get by on the con. She lived mainly by the revolving door trick—taking a man back to an expensive hotel and asking him to wait outside while she checked up and booked a room. The punter never liked to appear ungenerous and usually gave her twenty pounds or so. Then she walked past the desk and straight out of a service door into a sidestreet.

Once she was stoned and made the mistake of doing it to the same man twice, finding him leaning by the side door when she split. But Jane could talk her way out of most things and borrowed another tenner off him on the strength of her story. If she was suddenly short of money for a few packets she often walked into the Hilton, asked for her key—any key—and turned the room over.

She had nerve for twenty-one years of age. Underneath she was frightened silly. One night we were making love when she started to weep, as she had done before. Towards the end the tears became hysteria, blank terror in the darkened room until she fainted. . . . The Fear.

A big Chinese habit was a crushing burden but often a short-lived one, for trouble with the police was just a shot away. It often came as a relief; and withdrawal from Chinese was never as bad as with English smack.

I cruised through the months as part of the crowd. . . . The West End became known to me in all its differing moods, dirty but relatively innocent during the day—away from the Street at least—its edges blurred by the swarming office girls and the dust and traffic exhausts. In the evenings it became the land of hope, the bustling crowds looking for the answers to their needs, the lighter ones like the films and plays, the darker side as the crowds broke down into individuals looking for a boy, or a whore, somewhere to get fucked or beaten. Night-time, before the water wagons came round again, was the sinister, spent period—drunks lying in doorways, their money gone, the occasional flash of violence outside one of the clubs, blood in the road. . . . Walking from Covent Garden, away from the coffee stall under the Inigo Jones church, the birds starting to sing at five in the morning . . . down the hill to Charing Cross, the delivery vans and lorries a reminder of more peaceful lives . . . looking out over the river, steel-grey and silent . . . I was a long way from home.

I walked into Annette in the early morning, almost knocking her over as I rounded the corner into Coventry Street. She was waiting to meet a connection. We walked around together for a while, talking most of the time not so much as old acquaintances or ex-lovers, but as two junkies. She was now very thin; but her beauty was still there, her eyes enormous in her white, fine-boned face.

The eyes showed a hopelessness I had come to recognize, although her conversation was optimistic. The optimism seemed unreal, I thought. At seventeen Annette had seemed a sophisticated woman. Now she looked lost. For much of the time we talked of the present rather than the past, of her plans for a cure, of her fiancé. I knew the fiancé, a sensitive and friendly Australian, but so crushed by junk and hopelessness that he was catatonic for hours at a time.

We turned into the park and talked of Julia and Angie, Angie who had stayed with Annette the last time she was in England and who had got hooked herself, probably, I reflected, dating back to when she had visited Mike and myself in hospital. But she had been lucky enough to split and get clear, while Annette was sinking. . . .

'The seed was always there,' said Annette quietly.

'And if you hadn't lived with me?'

She shrugged her shoulders. It was a stupid question to ask anyway, incapable of answer. We walked along in silence, looking at the ducks on the lake, watching the sun glittering behind the spires and turrets of Whitehall.

It was time for Annette to meet her dealer. I wanted to stop the clock, to make love to her there in the park, wanting to bridge the years and events with bodies not words, to try and annihilate our past and her tragedy. . . .

But it was too late; and Annette had to see the Man. So we walked back to the steps leading out of the park and into the West End, kissing each other goodbye.

12

One of the places I had crashed at earlier in the year was a small charitable centre for junkies. It operated out of an old and cavernous building in the heart of Soho and was run at that time by a couple of old ladies—rather the tea-and-buns type—and one full-time psychologist. In the comparative peace and comfort of its offices I could take an uninterrupted fix or snatch some sleep.

I had come to know the psychologist separately. He was a curious chap. Tall and good-looking, wearing dark glasses all the time, he had a personality that was hard to grasp; somehow he eluded one. In his late thirties, a man of warmth and drive, he lived in one of the cramped and dusty flats in Gerrard Street, a place with an atmosphere all its own. I often stayed there as well, and grew to like Rupert. But it was impossible to know whether he was a saintly figure who made no distinctions, either between his social life and his work, his friends, his clients and his enemies—or whether he was devoid of any moral sense at all.

He was a Marxist homosexual, the most noticeable features of his flat being the books and the boys. The books rambled on rickety shelves all over the pad, volumes on radical psychiatry, social history, trade union reform, tattered piles of professional journals, stacks of the old Left Book Club editions. The boys took up less space but made more noise. There were always two or three of them there and sometimes more—one of them Rupert's lover of the moment, the others (twittering theatrical aspirants, hard cases with tattoos, occasional transvestites) there to ask Rupert's advice on their latest problems or to take refuge for a day or so. They looked up to him like younger brothers.

The whores who lived there looked up to him as well, tough Glasgow girls usually, who shopped and tidied in the together way that prostitutes often have. If one of them left or got arrested then another, from the same milieu, took her place.

Rupert's flat was one of the centres of classical Soho life. Somehow, by the strength of his personality, he kept a semblance of order amongst the crowds, the older generation represented by Beggars' Opera villains and West End eccentrics, bearded figures, intellectuals, emigrés writing their memoirs of Budapest in the thirties.

Through Rupert I entered the world of the 'helper', the network of charitable workers, probation officers, kindly do-gooders and career-minded social workers. Perhaps the junk field was the wrong area in which to witness their efforts: in other, more amenable, fields their attempts might have given a more positive impression. Confronted with junkies they seemed futile, pursuing phantasms of their own creation.

But then the whole idea of helping people for a living, for a career, seemed strange and unnatural to me, the attempt to turn human warmth into a marketable commodity and a structured profession. And Rupert, a sinner himself, was able to give more and communicate more naturally with the lost youngsters around him than any of the orthodox professionals I met subsequently. . . . Christ himself had no degree qualifications.

Rupert's ability to work with others, loose and spontaneous as it was, diminished once he exchanged his flat and the Soho streets for the offices of the drug charity and a circumscribed role. But somehow I got drawn into the same game; for having seen me hanging about with my habit for months, he asked me to work with him. I agreed, somewhat reluctantly but tired of looking at my own arms, and I worked there for the next year or so, irregularly at first, full-time as the place expanded, taking over the management of the centre when Rupert resigned in early 1969.

I was in flight from my own ego anyway, bored and impatient with my own problems. Perhaps I felt some faint sense of obligation—or rather loyalty—to my own kind. Possibly it was just something to do. In any case it was an interesting period, witnessing—amongst other things—the attempts of human beings, most of them living in a moral vacuum themselves, to help and guide others.

Originally the charity had been set up to offer mutual aid

and assistance to the families of addicts, an extreme example of the indirect approach. But Rupert had grafted an aid and advice centre onto the structure and, under the impact of the huge numbers of addicts wanting help, the tail tended to wag the dog. Of course the place was absolutely riven by disputes and battles over policy. Charities, after all, have no means of measuring their own validity so anything can happen, depending on the will and personality of the individuals concerned. An uneasy peace was maintained between the different factions.

Under the influence of the two of us, the charity evolved into a simple service for drug addicts, neither more nor less. Addicts came to seek a doctor, a clinic, food, clothing or just a bed for the night—we found it for them. If they wanted a cure we fixed up a hospital bed; but otherwise we weren't concerned with reduction or withdrawal. Our role was simply to give them what they asked for if it was within our powers.

With my rather black-and-white outlook this seemed a very sensible way of doing things, but we were working in a minefield. Assisting junkies in this way had rather different connotations from working with handicapped children or spastics. Nobody seemed to be sure if they should be helped at all unless such help was geared to getting them away from junk. And help without strings. . . ?

'Do you mean to say that help is given on demand?' enquired a shaken female probation officer, one of the mass of visitors who called in to study our methods, 'that you don't work on a basis of reciprocity?'

I explained patiently that the eventual destiny of the addict lay in other hands, perhaps even those of the addict himself.

'And they can help themselves to food and walk straight out?' I nodded, yes, I was afraid they could do that too. She lapsed into silence and puzzlement. Occasionally I lost patience and ended all confusion by dropping the item that I was an addict myself. A subtle change in response, an explanation of our irresponsible methods. . . .

It might have been wiser to have kept our methods to ourselves. But it was difficult to do so, as we got drawn into the network of institutions and achieved rather a lot of publicity as we grew. There was a stream of callers—professionals, research workers, academics looking for answers, the mass media seeking stories. The drug scene was very visible at this time and we worked in the glare. Inevitable but foolish: you don't help people by broadcasting it, you simply do it. Perhaps one shouldn't even write about it.

My own role was a curious one, the more so after Rupert resigned and my influence became uncomfortably conspicuous. I was part of the addict culture myself, no wiser than the rest about ultimate answers, but putting on my administrator's hat during the day and dealing as a concerned individual with the hospitals, the probation service, police and courts. I felt a little like an imposter, uncertain whose side I'd be on if I had to choose.

The organization grew at an alarming speed in response to demand and to Parkinson's Law. By early 1969 the little venture in Soho had turned into an unwieldy institution working from new and larger premises at an increased rent, and using the services of forty part-time volunteers as well as five or six permanent staff. The funds required grew commensurately. The operation had been run on a few pounds a week; soon it was costing six thousand a year. And that meant more fund-raising, more selling of the operation, more assistance from the City and wealthy foundations.

I watched this cancerous growth with mounting distaste. I had little loyalty to any organization, much less to charities, dedicated as they were primarily to their own continued existence, least of all to a charity which grew to resemble an infantry division—the personnel increasing the further back one went from the scene of the action. Yet it was difficult to turn one's back.

Confronted with the realities of mass drug abuse, rather than elitist, minority drug use, I had to question a few of my own ideas. There wasn't a lot of evidence for free will here, not many signs of personal quests. The middle classes were deserting addiction in droves, scared off by the horrid problems of getting regular supplies: the vicious Chinatown scene or the clinics with their atmosphere of social security offices. They turned to irregular snorting, making massive efforts to avoid developing a habit instead of diving straight into one as they had in the past.

What we began to see were hordes of lost and misguided young men from the factories and council estates, kids out of orphanages, depressed hard cases apparently lacking much choice in anything. And the late casualties of flower power, people confronted with a colder world than the dreams of 1967 and easy acid had prepared them for.

Anyone who was reasonably together phoned us up, used our services and split. The rest remained: a huge and unruly crowd of stumbling victims, milling in and out of the kitchen, taking a fix in the corner, nodding off or arguing and fighting among themselves. Not a pretty sight, little romance here, especially as many of them had taken to injecting all varieties of rubbish into themselves in the face of the junk famine and rising prices: barbiturate capsules, dexedrine capsules, methadone tablets, suspicious-looking Chinese.

Once the place had grown to this size, and once it started to gain an institutional atmosphere—as was inevitable—I knew I would have to turn my back and leave. I was never the right man for formal work with drug addicts, uninterested in joining the boom industry of helping junkies and unable to believe in the myths that surrounded the scene.

Besides, I had strange ideas about the sanctity of the human spirit and the immorality of attempts to invade it. I might have been right, but as we attracted greater and greater numbers of drug users rather than pure junkies—users who shot into their arms just about anything within reach, who often no longer knew their own name, the question became academic, the spirit and will untraceable.

Helping users like that meant looking down on them and taking their decisions for them: I could not do that. There were many others around who could. I stood at the back of our hall one evening and listened to the smiling doctor reading his paper on 'Leucotomy as a treatment for drug dependence' and reciting the details of the brains he had cut. Whatever side I was on, I reflected, it wasn't that one.

Gerry walked into the office late one morning. I was surprised to see him, knowing that he had been cured, not expecting to see him near junk centres again. He hadn't changed a lot in appearance—a little tighter and older around the mouth, the juvenile-delinquent look gone. I grinned and made a gesture encompassing the structure around me:

'Where we purge our past. . . . Let's go out and get a cup of coffee.' We walked through the crowded Soho streets, fresh and bustling at this time of day, until we found a place where we could talk. We had seen each other irregularly since our row in Fulham; the last I had heard was that he had gone to live in Greece with Rosalind. I asked what had happened.

'I've just come out of prison. The colonels put me away for eighteen months for possession of pot, a kilo of hashish.' He turned his mouth down in the rueful way he had. No complaints.

And now?

He gave a laugh, outside himself. 'I seem to be getting hooked again.'

'But where's Rosalind?'

'She came back when I got busted. I haven't seen her.' Another scene that was clearly over.

'Jesus Christ,' I said, 'I thought you'd been off all this time, Gerry; you were the success story. . . .'

He told me of the last few years, about his cure, about Rosalind, Greece, the past. I found it hard to listen; so sure had I been that Gerry was free of stuff, that in spite of his weaknesses he was the one with the overall strength to make it. But then strength alone wasn't enough. Looking at him it was impossible to know what he felt: he always discussed misfortune as if it was someone else who had suffered. The mask was still in place.

Just once I had seen something of what went on deep behind his defences. The noise in the streets outside, Gerry's voice, the Italianate clatter around us faded into the distance, as I thought back to the black comedy that had been our last meeting.

My flat, Julia, Angie, a couple of friends, all of us near the end of an acid trip. The doorbell rang, reverberating through the room. Gerry arrived and after the briefest of conversations I invited him to join us, turning him on to his first taste, powerful American blotting-paper acid.

For an hour he sat quietly on a couch, eyelids drooping, while the rest of us jabbered incessantly. Then something made me look at him more closely than before, noticing the tension in the man for the first time, watching a flood of feeling trying to burst its way out. He started laughing, softly at first, then more and more loudly and violently until an enormous spasm carried him off the couch and onto the floor, rolling across the carpet like an egg, coming to a teetering rest and then rolling all the way back again, legs tucked into his body.

The paroxysms continued for ten or fifteen minutes. But, appallingly, every time he drew breath between the bursts and at the end of a roll, his face turned utterly and grotesquely tragic, the mouth drooping madly at the corners, the eyes filling with tears, like a gargoyle. Slowly he began to calm down; but his face did not revert to normal—the masks that appeared were those of Athenian drama, stupidly funny, dreadfully sad by turns. I had never believed that Gerry possessed much real sadness.

Later we trooped out into the evening and ended up, ludicrously, in a Kensington wimpy bar. Most of us were on our way down and half-sober by then; but Gerry was far, far away. He seemed more and more tragic and vulnerable, utterly homeless and without roots, inconsolable in spite of our efforts, reminding each of us of the eternal Wandering Jew.

The rest of us opted for hamburgers. Gerry thought long and hard, and in a tired and weary voice chose some apple pie, telling us that he envied our healthy meat but felt he had no choice. When it arrived he fixed it with a mixture of expressions and debated whether to have some cream. Finally he made his decision and the waiter was summoned, duly appearing with one of those nasty stirrup-pump affairs that they froth the cream in. One by one we stopped eating, ceased conversation and looked at Gerry.

He no longer knew who he was. But with his natural gift for mime which emerged without conscious control, and with something else, something beyond himself, he transfixed us without words, staring again at the apple pie and back at the lusty immigrant waiter looming over him with the cylinder. Into the sad and window-shrunken pastry he projected himself, making us believe it was he, that his fate was inexorably bound up with the pie.

'I think,' he said very quietly, 'I think I'll have just a little cream please.' We sat motionless, aware of some imminent disaster.

The waiter looked at him, grinned broadly and pumped his machine. A flood of puffy ectoplasmic stuff spurted out, coiled, heaped and spiralled obscenely—and obliterated the apple pie beneath it. I shivered and leaned back, my hands to my face. Gerry spoke like a man on the scaffold, with an effort at control.

'It might have lived,' he told the bemused waiter, 'and you have destroyed it for ever.' Angie burst into tears, the others sat there stunned. Gerry, his fate sealed, visible to all, broke into laughter again, a cold and lonely laughter echoing through my head. . . .

Gradually I returned to the present and to the surroundings of the Amalfi patisserie. Gerry had fallen silent. I stared hard at him, remembering how I had once so envied his strength and apparent invulnerability.

'We're both getting older,' I said tritely. 'If you get hooked again now you might not have another chance.'

'Worse things can happen.' Subject closed. 'What about you?'

'I don't know. But I'm thinking of coming off again.'

'Why?'

Hard to put into words, especially with the memory of a cured Gerry and his apple pie in front of me.

'Because there's nowhere for me to go any longer. And I can't resign myself to stuff.' There was a pause. 'Once I thought that junk put something in my hands, an essence, something I could grasp—' I made a gesture to try and express it. Gerry nodded understanding. 'It was like holding time. And there was always more of that feeling to chase. But it was slipping away while I was still looking for it.'

'You're still hooked,' Gerry, the realist, pointed out.

'I know, that doesn't slip away. And I still don't know how to cope with it.'

We talked more before leaving. I learnt to my amusement that Gerry was staying at Rupert's until he knew where he was going to. Then we parted and I walked back to work, saddened at Gerry's relapse, aware that there was no advice I could give him; there were no magic words.

I must be going soft, I thought, this concern for others. Each of us had his own life, it was up to each of us what we did with it. It was foolish to get the horrors, even for friends. One couldn't be responsible for everyone.

Other old friends appeared at the charity offices, sometimes to see me, occasionally seeking help or else looking to score. Seeing them from that perspective provided a graph of their decline, in parallel with my own. Most of us had found things slipping through our fingers in one sense or another, the carelessness of the sixties taking on a darker hue.

Phil Seamen often staggered in. He never changed very much either; his body had taken so much punishment earlier in life that further damage hardly showed. He could have been anywhere between forty-five and sixty years of age. He was still working, philosophical about the young musicians he had trained and who had now overtaken him, walking unhurriedly towards his inevitable end.

And Steve, another musician, sometimes called in when he was in town. He was more embittered than Phil, bewildered by the way his brilliance had gone relatively unrewarded while all the other members of his band had gone on to world fame. But then Steve had come from a different generation, and had believed that the gates were opening to him with a music that nobody else had ever played.

He had spent a year in America trying to stay off, had watched his marriage and career disintegrate under him and was now trying to start again, hooked once more. I went to a couple of his concerts and came away depressed: the fire and attack in his playing were gone. At his peak, playing the 'acid rock' he had introduced, there had been a marvellous sense of conquest and direction, a liberation of unknown territory that had mirrored the hopes of many of us. Now I heard confusion and mystical yearning; the music lacked conviction, just as Steve and the rest of us now did.

But away from work I avoided most of the users I had known in the past, aware that the scene was dead to me, oppressed by the way so many had come to grief. Most of the time I lived at my brother's in a junk-tinged parody of a quiet working life, mixing with a few of the younger junkies whom I hadn't known in the beginning, having sporadic affairs with some of the more attractive and less neurotic female users who appeared in junk territory, users who still had most of their illusions untouched. Much of my free time I spent in reference libraries, studying endless literature about consciousness, psychology and the self.

For what I had told Gerry had been true enough. I was thinking of making another attempt at coming off. There really couldn't be any place else to go: just this gradually shrinking life in a slowly shrinking organism. But this time I intended to avoid some of my past mistakes, knowing that it would be a long path with no guarantees. I wasn't even considering hospital cures or abrupt withdrawal, knowing I would doom myself that way to repeat the old patterns, replace the sickness with emptiness, give myself freedom with nothing to free.

There was clearly something missing in the ways that I and others had tried—assuming that it was possible to come off at all. The desire to get off, 'motivation' as the doctors called it, obviously wasn't enough; most junkies who tried to stop had the desire. And the daily parade of failure and despair in Soho, the constant impression of blindfolded men missing a doorway, reinforced my belief that existing techniques were worthless. Somewhere there was a basic flaw in approach, a whole area that we were ignoring.

One could never go back, that was clear enough. Cures predicated on a subtraction of junk and an uncovering of the old, 'normal' personality were almost bound to fail; that I did know. Nobody remained the same, junk or no junk, and besides, the whole realm of drug addiction was bound to modify almost everything in one's previous character. The first question was to try and find those parts of oneself that could be worked on. The second: how could one build something new, something to transcend the destruction and fragmention liberated by heroin? Most 'cures' seemed like extensions of drug addiction, in the sense that a continuing battle with a postulated self was expected. Did that conflict have to exist at all? Or were the terms false?

I spent the months thinking this way, looking for guidelines, before attempting to cut down a single pill.

It was hard not to be disheartened by others' lack of success. Of all the addicts I had known with large-scale habits—and English habits, with the strength and purity of the gear, were something altogether more serious than the American or Continental variety—not one was known to me as a definite cure; Gerry had been the nearest. There had to be some others, I reasoned, people who weren't seen because they no longer wanted anything to do with junk and junkies.

But where were they? Out of the scores and scores of hard core users I had known very well, only a few could not be accounted for. People disappeared all the time. Many of them were later found to be dead or in prison. Others surfaced after a gap of many months, standing in Piccadilly trying to score, slumped out in some addict's flat, evasive and distant-eyed, unwilling to discuss their failure, or simply blank.

There was no-one, no fund of information to draw strength from, nobody even to say what was possible. Most books about junk were either written from the other side of the hill, by outsiders, or by obvious charlatans. I remembered the only book I had seen by a genuine addict from a cured perspective, some sort of trashy claim, like 'I Returned from the Dead'. Later I met the author, standing sweat-stained and dirty, his clothes in tatters, waiting for his script in Boots. I believe it was the love of a good woman that saved him.

On the other hand medical literature was a refined exercise in unreality, spiralling away into areas unknown to me, sets of theories searching for a centre. By now I had met most of the doctors in the field and had the chance to talk to them . . . I remembered the way my heart had sunk the first time that one of them, the author of several studies in addiction, started asking me—me—if I could give him any clues.

'It's no good asking me,' I yelped, 'I thought you were going to tell me the answers.'

The feeling of being on one's own again. . . .

But then this ultimate isolation had been implicit in my first experiences with junk, had been part of the challenge that attracted me. Pointless to complain now, I thought. Only I had lost much of the youthful arrogance and certainty that I had once possessed, the belief that I could trespass where others feared to walk. Now I looked around and wondered if I could succeed where so many had failed. And could I possibly deserve to? But that was the wrong question to ask.

In trying to find an approach through study and investigation, I was confronted with the same problems that I had been unable to resolve years before: we had no dependable methods of working on the self. Between the academic constructs of the psychiatrists and the clogged mysticism of

Sandy and the other acid freaks there was no middle way that I could use. The people with the theories rarely had the insight; those with the experience lacked control and any sense of rigour. Gradually I worked out what was required even to begin. I needed more than theories and more than my own and others' chaotic and undirected efforts at exploration of reality; I needed some science and a map. A science of the self and a map of the mind.

Like others before me I had to turn to older models, renewing an interest in Eastern psychological theory. But then this was common sense—after all, the energies of the Indians and Tibetans had been devoted to studying the mind and its existence while we had been occupied with other things. It was logical to suppose that they would know more. And my experience with acid had provided a certain confirmation, in the sense that whole areas of the mind and states of consciousness that were lumped together as meaningless, or 'the unconscious', could be matched up fairly well with some of the phenomena that Eastern theories and practice postulated.

But while studying, I had reservations. Since the mid-sixties people I knew had been devoting themselves to Yoga or esoteric Buddhism. But their experiences had seemed to lead them away from their surroundings rather than to any unification; it was hard to integrate Eastern mystical ideas or practice with life in a modern Western country.

And, intuitively, I felt that it might be wrong to try and import a science and a way of seeing from lands and cultures thousands of miles away, to try and superimpose the outlook of a distant minority and a different race onto a European head. A view of reality, a mode of operating in the world, was not the same as the Afghan coats and patchouli oil that youngsters brought back along the hippy trail. Even supposing that one got results, the end product was likely to be some sort of mutant, someone in true touch with neither culture.

And another, more immediate difficulty. How could one sort out the scientific parts of the disciplines from the cultural accretions and superstition that surrounded and permeated them? It had taken me long enough to penetrate some of our home-grown myths and untruths. I had never even been to the East. How would I ever develop the discrimination?

I had one great advantage: I had no romantic preference for another culture, no fashionable illusions and predispositions; I was only looking for tools and methods as means to an end.

If Eastern esoteric approaches were based on a reality, if they dealt in things that worked, then the foundations could surely be sought from other directions. Esoteric techniques appeared to offer the chance of a total view of the mind, and also methods of working on the self. It was a matter of finding the right ones.

13

It would soon be time to move. I wrote to Dale and asked him to take me back as a patient while I cut down, unwilling to depend on the whims and idiocies of my other clinic. We worked out a tentative scheme: I would see him once a fortnight and reduce the script by a pill or so at a time. It would take at least a year.

Dale was the right man, one of the very few doctors on the junk scene with no front, no artificiality and no obvious hang-ups of his own. His only 'failing' as a psychiatrist in Cane Hill had been the mild hero-worship he attracted, the patients depending on his judgement rather than their own more than he wanted them to. He did have an intensely irritating habit of forgetting to put requested increases onto the scripts—a habit which it was impossible ever to be sure about. Was he just absent-minded, or was that his way of refusing or delaying the matter? One never found out, subsequent references to such incidents being met with surprise or innocent ignorance. But apart from the rages that this caused—useless for the disappointment was somehow never discovered until Dale had vanished—I never knew an addict with a single word to say against him. In the junk field that was something truly remarkable.

At the beginning of 1970 events at the charity precipitated my departure. I knew I couldn't stay there anyway with my own head to look after. But the decision was taken for me when yet greater financial needs necessitated bringing in outsiders to put up money and help establish the place on a firmer footing. They didn't like the way I worked and, understandably from their point of view, didn't want an addict in sole charge any longer.

So I resigned. I had been no better than the other, straight workers in the field, my motives no purer. Perhaps an uneasy conscience at having sold stuff, at having profited from the scene in the past, had led me to stay as long as I had, paralleling in a darker way the materially induced guilt of the comfortable middle classes who dominated such work. It was suggested to me before I left that I might want to return to the work after giving up junk. I shook my head.

'No,' I said, 'I don't think so. I was just passing through.'

With the initial aid of a loan from another of the people I had worked with, I withdrew to my brother's place once more, there to become the hermit, or mystic, of Upper Norwood, a distracted and unlikely figure. But I had found my map and I set out to use it.

'Conventional' methods of dealing with drug addiction were out, both because of their inadequacy in practice and because of my own unwillingness or inability to accept their terms of reference. Broadly speaking there were two main ways that an addict could try and get 'cured' in concert with others, and with outside help. Both involved accepting new interpretations of past behaviour and ways of thinking.

The psychiatric method involved accepting one's past actions as pathological and seeking their origins in the mind and in early upbringing. Then there were the newer, socially oriented units that had sprung up for treating behavioural problems—the jargon once again—in England and America. Here the approach was quite different: a dismissal of the psyche and inner reality, a high-temperature stress on accepting that the addict was simply in need of learning, re-schooling, education. The word 'stupid' featured prominently in their vocabulary. Both methods could get some results. But then all methods—from orgone boxes to tree therapy—could get results depending on the stage that the client or patient had reached.

There wasn't a lot to be said in favour of the second method. Its interest lay more in the insight it gave into the truly confused state of American social theories than in any validity it might possess. I interviewed one of the founders of an important unit on the US West Coast to find out something about the set-up. What was the cure rate?

'Well, we don't like to talk about cure until a good time has elapsed and the addict is functioning in the community again. And we've only been going a few years.'

But how many cures?

'Well it's high, about thirty per cent. But we can't be sure, because they don't leave. They stay in the unit and work with us.'

And this was with the milder American habits, usually very short-term ones.

'How long do they stay?'

'Some of them have been there with us for five years. Some have set up their own units.'

Funny sort of cure. But the practitioners had stumbled on some valuable old knowledge: any complete rejection of one's past, the more hysterical the better, could liberate powerful, if transient energies, the pattern of converted Christians and reformed sinners since time began. Sustaining the crusade was the problem, which was why so many of them went into the cure business themselves—wild-eyed and rather fanatical young men who talked of mind games, truth kicks, evasion and reality trips.

The psychiatric approach offered the chance of a deeper, less fragile result, and the possibility of retaining a sense of humour about the world, something manifestly lacking in the other crowd, although it was quite obvious that neither the therapist nor the patient in fact understood the tools or forces that they were attempting to manipulate. But the methods had been evolved for dealing with cases of gross psychological delusion; they could not easily be applied to drug addiction where the basis of behaviour could be considered pathological while the day-to-day manifestations were quite rational. Furthermore psychiatry, in general, worked in a vacuum, the question of one's relation to society being evaded. Socially the aim was said to be the classical Freudian one: the ability to function. But to function as what?

It wasn't simply that I disagreed with orthodox, post-Freudian ideas or that I disliked psychiatrists. My whole position was dictated by the fact that my experiences had shown the present state of knowledge to be glaringly inadequate and in certain respects simply untrue, based as it largely was on an attempt to squeeze unknown areas and phenomena into a medical or 'scientific' framework. The whole concept of the 'unconscious' was of little value to me, for what good was it to be told of its existence in terms of a complete inner mystery akin to the Matto Grosso? I needed to know the pathways, the sources of energy, the different relationships between the parts.

But perhaps more important than these objections—for no doubt exceptions could be found, therapists who understood more than their theories indicated, loophole units like Cane Hill—was my own unwillingness to accept a 'cure' on anyone else's terms. Through arrogance, inflexibility or misguidedness I was unable to jettison the past and reinterpret it according to other people's models.

I still had no faith in the society from which I sprang. In 1963 I had believed that that society was on a collision course, and perhaps junk use had been tied up with my own feelings of inability to change or influence things. Nothing had happened to make me change my mind. Indeed the evidence had become more visible, so that my views which at one time had been outside the framework of debate were becoming more widespread.

Not all pessimists became junkies, certainly. But the deep-rooted pessimism in me, coloured and strengthened by the junk experience, was no firm basis for integration, no foundation for saying: 'My views were mistaken, my behaviour was invalid and self-destructive; help show me where I went wrong.' For it was based not on any ideology or political stance, but on a deep antipathy to our ways of seeing the world, the ways of psychologists included.

Running through all my experiences with drugs, an unstressed theme, had been the attempt to break out of our ways of seeing. Drugs, drugs rather than just junk, had offered the chance of stepping outside our normal vision, outside the framework of our time and place, a framework decided for most of us without our knowledge or control. Amidst all the adolescent escapades and self-indulgence, underneath the Rimbaudian attempts 'to see by making the self monstrous', I had possessed a curious sense of purpose. And if the price of getting cured was the rejection of that purpose and that vision, then it truly wasn't worth it.

But the result, of course, had been failure. Apparently absolute and unqualified failure in my own terms. It didn't matter if it was suggested that I used junk because I wanted to make love to my mother and kill my father, that I had a breast-fixated need for immediate sensual gratification, that I could not adjust, that I was riven by conflict. None of these things mattered, because they could never be decided for certain and meant nothing to me. What was important was that I had lost my way: in stepping outside I had ended up with a vision dominated by need, focussed on the end of my nose, a way of life that was finally static.

There was no way back. I had to find a new way for myself, accepting the failure that I understood, accepting the fact that junk had subverted my will. Given the tools and the guidelines I believed that it could be done.

It was unrealistic to suppose that one could simply discard all the bits of oneself that were 'undesirable' or unproductive. But they could be, I thought, rechannelled if one knew where one had gone wrong. And those aspects of myself and my behaviour that weren't necessarily integral, but had been liberated and nourished by the junk experience, could be brought back into an operating network. If I could never get the lid back on that Pandora's Box, I could at least learn to live with the errant creatures, see them for what they were. Somewhere underneath the debris I might rediscover the will and find a way of redirecting it so that it no longer swung back upon me like a scorpion's tail.

Over the last eighteen months I had gradually been assembling the elements of a system of my own. My first priority had been to find a tradition of working on the self which made sense of the territory I had already uncovered and which would parallel Eastern methods without their disadvantages. The long periods in the libraries had been spent studying European mysticism.

I had remained aloof from the fashionable immersal in fringe subjects such as astrology, magic and the various forms of mysticism, uninterested in ushering in the Age of Aquarius and only too aware of how such pursuits could degenerate into a narrow escapism—especially when they were taken up, as they usually were, in a vapid and uncritical way. But in one or two respects I had changed my mind, for the varieties of European mysticism appeared to provide the basic parallels I was looking for.

Studying it critically was not easy. For while one could go into any specialist bookshop or good library and obtain clear and scientific manuals on Yoga, the product of many hundreds of years of disciplined teaching, the European mystical tradition was neither clear nor accessible, was in fact a forest of nonsense, beauty, obscurity and confusion which defied description.

But certain things were clear. There was a vast Western literature of mysticism and occult psychology with discernible—after an effort—patterns and aims, unconcerned with mental 'sickness' or 'health' but only with the development of consciousness. The material was divorced from any mainstream, however; firstly because writers shrouded their work in secrecy and complex symbolism, successfully concealing much of the sense of what they had to say even from their contemporaries; and additionally because the whole point of their work was somehow divorced from our present ways of seeing—if it was noticed at all it was seen as a curiosity or a puzzling irrelevance save for the religious-minded.

This alien quality of the subject caused me problems: it required an effort of will to make sense of the writers' aims, and the fact that they were either ignored by the majority or else fervently defended by committed commentators led to a strange disorientation, an absence of intellectual ground under my feet. And whilst I was involved in a serious venture I was also uncomfortably aware that I was rubbing shoulders with the flat-earthers, the flying saucer freaks and the 'cheque book gypsies', rich young men who lived in caravans and muttered about Glastonbury and the Grail— people, in short, who would believe anything as long as it was mysterious. Alchemy, which I studied with some care, exemplified the difficulties.

Alchemy? People were likely to be bemused or sympathetic if they found out I was interested in the subject. Current opinion stated that it was simply a primitive form of science, valuable perhaps for its incidental chemical discoveries, but essentially a joke subject in these enlightened times.

And yet it was quite obvious that many alchemical texts were nothing to do with the making of physical gold but used the process as a metaphor to describe psychological phenomena. The basic alchemical sequence, for example, the way in which the 'matter' being worked on was seen to change from black to white to red, while apparently relating to the alchemist's workshop and materials, was clearly concerned with the development of consciousness, the colour symbolism signifying the different stages that the mind could reach.

Unfortunately the recondite and bizarre symbolism that all alchemists used meant that most of their secrets were safe from me as well, for while I could understand the broad aim of their work its details defeated me, like others before. Nor was the situation helped by the facts that plenty of alchemists actually had been trying to make gold and that the discipline had been infiltrated by numberless charlatans and con-men through the centuries.

While I had to give up on strictly alchemical works, wishing they had either said more or stayed silent, I continued with the study of the related ideas of occult and hermetic psychological theory, and these tended to confirm the broad picture.

Some of the psychoanalysts who had so often drawn my wrath were aware of the validity of the European occult tradition. Jung, in particular, had made deep studies of alchemical and related mysticism and had attempted to integrate the results into modern theory, not always successfully. And an earlier analyst, Silberer, had drawn similar, perhaps deeper, parallels. Their work provided a bridge to the past.

So by the time I decided to try and stop using junk I had a reasonable, though no doubt superficial, knowledge of occult psychology and the processes involved. Certain common factors recurred again and again. First, anyone who wished to gain access to the whole self and its relation to the world had to withdraw from outside interests and devote his entire attention to the mind. Then meditation and contemplation could lead to a hugely increased awareness and control of the psyche, a complete break with the past, a period of difficulty and perhaps despair (the 'blackness' of the alchemists) and the possibility of integration or super-awareness.

This programme, which has been classified by Jung as 'mystical introversion', was the one that I had tentatively decided to adopt. While its practice, in the past, had often shaded off into a religious quest—for which I felt myself unsuited—I felt that the process could be used for my own purposes, both as a way out of the junk trap and as a natural progression from it. Only I still lacked an accurate framework of the mind to operate with, a way of putting the scheme into action with some perspective and sense of location.

Partly by chance I began studying magic. From my reading it was clear that mystical introversion, the development of the self, overlapped with and sometimes deviated into straightforward magic, or the attempt to use the methods of consciousness-alteration for definite and worldly ends.

Steve, my favourite musician, had been the main advocate amongst my contemporaries of magically biased mysticism and the teachings of Aleister Crowley. I didn't particularly wish to follow him too closely for it seemed that the dangerous mix of magic and drugs had drawn him away from his art and into the shadows. But he had once given me some books on the Cabbala, which had lain, unread, for years; now I started reading and, fascinated by what I found, investigated more deeply.

Cabbalism, essentially the Jewish tradition of esoteric mysticism, had a giant body of literature and experience behind it and it differed from other occult studies in its practical, almost scientific approach to the mind. Here, I felt, was an analogue to Yoga, a tradition of comparable age and influence, which laid down definite guidelines to the unknown.

But I wasn't interested in becoming a magician. The few I had met were not impressive. There were the highly sinister ones, usually involved in a quest for power and wealth, often selling the results of their researches under the guise of 'self-development' courses to a wealthy and credulous public, and running their organizations in a repulsive and autocratic manner. Or there were the others, petty and rather suburban, opening temples in front rooms in Crouch End or Lichfield, poor minds, hung up with the sexual opportunities that group magic could offer. Steve was different, but confused and shrouded by now, lost in the territory that was eventually to kill him.

But the framework of Cabbalism, as against the uses to which it was put, meant something more to me. The entire basis of the scheme lay in a deceptively simple-looking hieroglyph—the Tree of Life. And here I felt that I was at last close to the map I had been seeking, for amongst other things—to put it mildly—the Tree was claimed to be a diagram of the hidden mind and its interactions. Of its constituent parts, one only, the most superficial, encompassed the entire Freudian unconscious.

There were ten of these parts or spheres: one conscious manifestation of personality and its physical body; one level of chaotic unconscious phenomena, a sort of mixing bowl of influences from the higher centres, heavily dominated by sexual thought and fantasy; and eight sources of life, behaviour and character, the upper three of which could never be reached directly, but only by inference. Each sphere had its own characteristics and all were necessary to the whole; but one in particular had special importance, for unlike the others it normally operated only intermittently and in relatively weakened form. This sphere was responsible for a true integration and humanization of the personality, and the attempt to bring it into active and continuous operation was one of the aims of practical Cabbalism.

Surrounding this core of the system was a massive body of magical and mystical doctrine—much of it easily accessible, for Crowley and his followers, having spent years collating older information and aligning it with Eastern systems, had published their results, ignoring the previous mystification and emphasis on secrecy. Their legacy was a clear but skeletal, morally neutral framework of the mind, open for anyone to investigate.

There was no scientific or strictly rational explanation of just how one could gain access to these 'objective' areas of the mind. Meditation, in its various forms, was considered a key route—but only if there was an initial willingness to accept the validity of the scheme and a powerful concentration on the work. The whole scheme was based on curious and alien concepts of mental energy, not explicable in modern terms. Meditation in some way opened up pathways, or imprints, the more effectively the more it was practised. This was fortunate—for while I was interested in meditation nothing was going to make me dress up in robes, hold my magical dagger and invoke spirits: my sense of the ludicrous was far too strong.

But why should some people gain access and not others? For the more one studied, the clearer it became that 'techniques' were not the key. In some people the head opened up, in others, however great their theoretical knowledge, nothing happened, the scheme remained a mental concept. The psychological make-up and previous experiences of any individual were obviously significant factors—as was a willingness or ability to open oneself to new perception. And this had to be backed up by a total determination. The older mystics had expressed the idea—given the *devotion* to what one wanted to achieve, the doors opened, independently of spirits, magical knowledge, daggers and pentagrams. And the process was always experiential, never to be reconciled with rational attempts to investigate it from the outside.

I lacked the devotion, in the strict sense, but I had a determination to know and to change, rather frightening in its intensity. And I had my past experiences—particularly my experiences with LSD. No-one is ever quite the same after taking acid, for better or for worse. And its operation is an analogue or microcosm of the mystical process, on a very short time span and with little conscious control—which is why the attempts of individuals to make sense of what happened on their trips read like unsophisticated mystical tracts. The knowledge gained from previous acid trips provided a bridge for me. And not in the sense that it had just provided me with experiences of temporary derangement: my own researches convinced me that acid worked directly on the important integrative sphere of the mind, in contrast to all other drugs. Junk, for example, opened up areas to exploration, but they were areas of darkness, not of light, or integration. A nice symmetry: acid helping to undo some of the damage that junk had wrought. . . .

So this was the system I made for myself—based on the writings of mystics from the past, some understanding, acquired with difficulty, of what they were trying to do and a tentative knowledge of the processes involved; a framework partially conceptual but apparently relating to verifiable, if subtle, phenomena—the framework of Cabbalism; a superficial knowledge of meditation passed on to me mainly by Steve, probably deriving from Yoga via Crowley; and some first-hand knowledge gained from consciousness-changing drugs—which I topped off with some ideas from the writings of Carlos Castaneda, who, whatever his sources, provided some valuable information on the relations between hallucinogens and mysticism or magic. A heady brew.

But was it a 'system' at all? In its patchwork quality it was almost a caricature of the modern Western mind in search of inner knowledge. Years later, a girlfriend of mine was describing her work in the local Yoga class—the physical Yoga, nothing heavy, which so many people take up. I listened to her describe how the class began with outline lectures on the gaining of concentration and the practice of the very simplest exercises; then she told me how any given position could be attained only after previous positions had been mastered; how she found muscles that she hadn't known existed—and then found out how to use them: a disciplined sequence and gradual progress, bit by bit.

Listening to the description with its obvious parallels to mental development and spiritual Yoga, I reflected ruefully on the contrast between her approach to the unused and unknown and my own scrappy and unguided collection of tools and influences—all without the equivalent of the Yoga teacher in the classroom, and which I put into practice with no preparation for the colossal areas of unknown territory that I was to encounter. I had a map, but in some respects it was unreliable: in any case it was like a military map, detailing some of the territory but giving no guarantee that one could ever get out again.

I had assembled these ingredients by early 1970. But I had made some serious mistakes. There was the obvious error that I was attempting to use forces that I couldn't really understand; and the idea that an essentially mystical process could be used as a way of giving up junk was both untested and highly debatable. In that sense it was magical, rather than mystical—an attempt at mastery instead of devotion. The records are full of what happens to people who make this attempt. Religious belief, moreover, in some way counters the chaos which any deep attempt at self-knowledge liberates; it is, in fact, a virtual necessity. I didn't have it. At the same time I was short-sighted and incautious—instead of asking myself how I would cope with new realities, I wasted my time wondering if anything would happen at all.

Nor did I really believe I would be a recluse for very long, let alone that the whole process would get utterly out of control, with a dynamic of its own, beyond my comprehension—analagous to the way that junk itself had stolen up on me while I thought I was the master. The cruellest twist of all was that while I gained the access I sought, this in itself could not resolve my addiction, indeed the conflicts involved in giving up stuff were magnified to enormous proportions. The consciousness expanded, I found my way to the centre of myself—and discovered that it was in chains, incapable of operating freely, bound by so many bonds that it was frightening to witness. For too much of the time that was the extent of the magical process—illumination of all the myriad difficulties with no definite methods of overcoming them, an experience foreshadowed by the very first acid trip I had taken years before. But this experience couldn't be switched off and I found myself with nowhere to retreat to.

For the rest of 1970 and the first few months of 1971 there is little to record by way of physical events. A diary would fill only a few pages. Most of the time I sat at home, meditated and wrote occasional, slightly insane poetry. At first this was by choice, later I felt that I had no option, caught inside the complex realms of my own mind, constricted by the bonds of illusion, hallucination and the apparently unending battle with the subverted self. Even my memory of the period is quite different from that of any other time: usually I have found my memory a precise and reliable instrument akin to a microscope, capable of being focussed or enlarged at will. For a period of over a year, I have no continuous memory at all, only episodes or reconstructed fragments.

The end result of the process goes beyond the bounds of this book. In the final chapters I describe the parts that are at all explicable and which relate to junk. For the rest, the temptation is always to say too much or too little and none of it can ever be verified. Still, I suppose it has to be said: this was the worst year of my life, a period of strange and unearthly dislocation, of flashes of past and present, of darkness and light, mostly darkness. And during it I hovered close to the answers I needed.

14

What began it all? There was no clear answer, no moment when I sat down and said: things will now change.

Having arranged the chemical side of withdrawal, the reduction, with Dale, I set out to sever most of the remaining routine links with the past and—as far as possible—with the junk world, preparing myself for a long period of virtual seclusion. I then began to meditate and contemplate often and regularly. And I threw in a 'technique' of my own invention: first questioning and then almost attacking the concept of my existing identity—how real was it, how valid under examination? This method, which I found easy to exercise in an increasingly ferocious fashion—better, as usual, at destruction than creation—combined with my increasing withdrawal from past patterns, probably provided the initial, necessary disorientation. Almost anyone, I suppose, who cut himself off from the visible evidence and structure of his identity and simultaneously questioned seriously the concept of that identity, would find odd things happening to him.

Within a few weeks I started to get the first, faint hints of an unknown dynamic coming into operation. It was as if a small but growing flame had been kindled into operation, or rather as if something had stirred slowly deep within, henceforth to have a volition of its own. A strange feeling this, slight but definite. The possibility that I might change my mind about it all faded.

Difficult to describe to others. And I'd never been good at saying goodbye.

'But where is it you're going to?' I was asked by a girl I'd been making a scene with. 'Abroad you mean?'

'I don't know,' I answered, slightly foolishly, staring over her shoulder, into the distance, 'I don't know. Geographically, probably nowhere; I'll still be at my brother's place for a while. It's difficult to explain.'

Later: 'I can't see it, I can't see that junk has such a hold on you now. I don't see the need.'

'Perhaps you romanticize me,' I told her. 'The junk need is as great as it ever was.' It was something more than junk that was pushing me, but I could hardly tell her what it was: I didn't know myself.

I stared past her again, out of the open window, thinking of, who was it, Geoff? Geoff. And the look on his face as he had moved into junk. Voyage in, voyage out. . . .

We walked to get her a taxi.

'I'd like to call you,' I said, 'but I don't know when, I don't think I'll be around for a while.'

'How long?'

But I didn't know that either.

I had read that the early stages of mystical introversion were attractive, seductive even, the mind beckoning the ego inwards, and down. I didn't find that: there was nothing seductive about my mind. Yet I was falling away, drifting inwards, my focus shortening. While I still hadn't cut myself off completely—I still had the daily trip to the chemist and I still saw some people socially, though in a rather superficial and preoccupied way—the outside world was becoming less and less important.

For what did it hold for me any longer? Only more of the same. I had no role to play any more whilst I still used junk, there was *nothing* further to know. And what could happen, what could I miss? There was nothing I would be needed for, I had no dependants. If any of the people I had said goodbye to were missing me, well, there was no need, I could only be less worthless to them in the future.

And if a man was walking the streets in search of me, with a cheque for a million pounds, what did it matter if I missed him? I could buy only junk and junk-related things with the money as I was. It was within that the action had to take place, it was my own head that had to change the reality and convert that cheque into a million pounds' worth of possibilities—instead of three sackloads of heroin: it was here that the outside world would be decided.

The scheme of the Tree made a significant difference to my early, internal wanderings. If I had possessed the other components of my 'system' but not the Cabbalistic framework, and if I had been told to sit down and meditate until my mind opened up, I wouldn't have had any idea where to start. Now I had my map and definite locations to search for, using specific symbols for particular spheres of the mind and meditating on them. The scheme was not a rigidly defined one and the results never tallied exactly with the theory, but the spheres provided beacons in the surrounding darkness. Also the pattern of the Tree had a curious *rightness* about it, a resonance hard to define

The access that I had sought became a reality and the phrase 'consciousness-expansion' a meaningful description: for during meditation I was able to 'move'—it was the only way to describe it—within the mind, and afterwards, in normal activity, the dimensions of conscious thought spread and enlarged as previously hidden processes came into open view and operation.

I had never been a person to oversimplify the mind. But I was amazed at the complexity of the inner world, everything a thousand times more complicated and interrelated than I had believed possible. Some new insight could appear, a connection between the centres or a relationship between an aspect of behaviour and the thought that had preceded it, hitherto unknown; and it could take days to unravel and bring to conscious, permanent understanding. And there were innumerable such connections to discover.

These difficulties applied to movement and discovery within any 'normal' mind. But to compound them I had the problem of the junk network: making sense of this secondary layer, trying to search out the threads and roots of addiction while attempting to cope with an expanding mental galaxy, sometimes brought me to the edge of exhaustion.

These changes, radical as they were, applied mainly to my personal, inner, world. But soon, only a couple of months after I had begun the process, outside contacts, such as they were, were affected: communication posed problems. The emphasis on symbolic thought and meditation and the strange insights this gave into the workings of language made conversation a new and problematic procedure, for words began to take on a curious character, every one seeming to mean a concatenation of hundreds of others and yet, under examination, possessing an unsatisfactory or partial relation to the thought behind it.

And soon afterwards another, perhaps connected, change: I began using my senses differently. In my encounters with others I paid less and less attention to the words they had to say, much more to the other, tenuous, signals that they emitted. Like many of the other changes that took place this wasn't something totally new or alien—for everyone, surely, felt intuitive reactions to other people, instant dislike, for example, or a vague feeling of discomfort or nervousness in someone's presence. But in my case these subtle and fleeting feelings became predominant and almost systematic: the vague, somatic connections between thought, reaction and feeling became open and enlarged, certain nerve centres reacted altogether more strongly and predictably than they ever had before.

I experimented with the source of the subtle signals, checking to see how others became aware of my presence and in what way. Control was sporadic and tenuous but I gained enough to be occasionally capable of making someone who hadn't seen me suddenly turn round to look.

This new sensitivity led in other directions as well and gave me some further clues to the operation of junk. For I found, under investigation, that whatever the nature of the signals to another person, they were inhibited or weakened by junk. The biological basis of attraction, repulsion, communication, was attacked at source by heroin.

It had been obvious to me that junk affected far more than the superficial levels of personality. But even though I knew that a person's *will* was turned against him, and while there had been other clues to the depths at which junk operated—the cessation of a woman's periods during a habit, for example, the dropping of a man's sperm count to near zero—I had never realized that the essential core of life was so radically affected.

Further inner research tended to confirm the evidence, the closer I approached to the centre. Yet this increasing awareness was apparently leading nowhere as far as of junk was concerned: the dimensions of the problem were becoming daily, and horrendously, more visible—but I knew no methods of altering the mind within and lacked any sense of growing mastery over junk. Rather late in the day I started running around, looking for more books.

In fact junk now began to assume an increasing importance. With all the changes that had taken place in these few months, with my past receding and my future obscure, junk was almost my sole evidence of identity and the continuity of existence. And worse: as my reduction began to bite, my body, which had hitherto been a quiet and reliable instrument of the process, began to suffer—and I understood why the mystics had always stressed the importance of a sound mind and body in the introspective venture.

Quite suddenly the contradictions in my plan were visible and having their effect: the process was distorted by a growing junk need. Under its pressure there began a fragmentation of my own purpose until what had started out as a conscious venture abruptly turned into a long nightmare. In its shadows I became the victim of a corrosive uncertainty, unsure of why I had begun the process, whether it had been my own free decision, or whether, like junk, it was running me.

The journey within went on, harassed by need but in an intense and all-embracing fashion, into territory that was often light years away from the conscious mind. Soon discipline, form, belief, diminished: my 'system' began to fail. Around this time the watchful eye began to cloud and the observing ego to break down. The walls were crumbling. And the record, for clarity's sake, has to be confined to those parts of the journey that covered the junk networks and the chemical embrace.

Something strange was happening to me. I forced my attention back to the face of the librarian. Why did I keep staring at his horrible dandruff? My field of view seemed to have altered, fixated on tiny details. . . . The man's voice forced itself back on my attention.

'. . . so I'm sure that we could get them for you. But these works aren't in demand here, really.' He paused and coughed. I was staring at the cuff of his jacket, at the tiny pieces of skin and dust that had gathered on the dark material.

'Fine, fine,' I answered, nodding my head, trying to remember what he had been saying, 'yes. Ah, I'd be grateful if you could.' Skin was very strange stuff once you actually looked at it, looked hard. Breaking up all the time.

'I'll come back tomorrow,' I said quickly. I wanted to get out of there.

I walked along the High Street, thinking. It wasn't a dizzy feeling or anything like that, I didn't feel intoxicated; it wasn't the sort of thing one could dismiss with a shake of the head. Tiredness possibly, I had been keeping some odd hours. I came to the big railway bridge over the road, noticing as I passed the rusting steel members, flecks of red oxide on the beams. I paused and stopped, looking at the peeling paint. It was like a race to stop the thing from crashing down, I thought: paint it, spray it, take the dirt off with a wire brush. Left to itself it would soon be eaten away. I stared at one corner, noticing the bubbling on the surface—and tore myself away.

I lay awake in bed that night wondering what was going on. A funny way to see things. To think of them that way, perhaps, to notice the odd detail—but to see them like that was strange.

The next day, walking up to get some breakfast, I looked around me carefully. It was the same world, nothing untoward had happened to it; it was still in place. The cars were still driving along, the people still walked, the shops were still selling, the walls were still standing. I paused, looking at the wall. One could see the bricks starting to flake very slightly. I walked over to the wall and had a closer look. No doubt about it, they were flaking. I rubbed my finger along the surface, miniature scraps of dirt and brickdust adhering to the skin. I turned and headed back home to get my dark glasses.

The break-up intensified over the next few weeks. Now, wherever I went I saw only people trying to stop themselves and their creations crumbling, shoring up a wavy, falling dam. The dust flaking off the edges of the paving stones, the woodwork inside houses beginning to warp and twist, the myriad bits and pieces in the air around me, detritus of worn clothing, rusting car bodies, wearing road surfaces. How much was real and what was I seeing that wasn't there? The bits of dust could be caught, held and identified, to the mystification of passers-by. They were real enough. But what of the passers-by themselves? I wondered why I could see skin flaking all over them, loosened eyelashes on the ends of their noses, hairs dropping out onto their collars.

And if the human debris was real, what about the way their faces changed from moment to moment? I was unsure of the continuity of anyone's identity any more. My own face in the mirror could seem strange to me.

Ripe as the situation was for humour, I was worried. Nothing could absolutely account for the changes. I was still receiving two grains of heroin or more and I hadn't cut down immediately before these events. Neither withdrawal nor an excess of junk could therefore be blamed. My health was good.

I didn't think that the introspective process alone could account for the changes directly, either; nothing on the map could quite identify what was going on. I was forced back on the explanation that in some mysterious way the changes in my own head, the partial loss of my old identity and my immersal in the mind were somehow being reflected in my whole perception of the outside world. At last I realized the potency of what I had been investigating.

The part of my mind which had built up over the years an impression—and essentially a necessary illusion—of firmness and stability in the world around me was beginning to lose, or relinquish, control. An announcement of change—the glass was shattering.

I recalled my experiences with acid. The early stages of a trip were fairly similar to what I was now experiencing—I thought of Julia's face and the way it changed from moment to moment. An acid trip was itself a temporary breakdown of identity and fixed ways of seeing. Perhaps this would be temporary, too.

But it lasted. The isolation which I had imposed on myself grew painful as I found it harder and harder to relate what was happening to me to the outside world. I still saw people occasionally but there was now an enormous gulf. Not so long after the walls began to crumble I was in someone's flat for an evening, smoking dope and talking to a group of people. The conversation strayed to the subject of perception. I described some of the puzzles I had been encountering, including the incidents with the walls, but I told the story lightly and for laughs.

It was met with stunned incomprehension. Followed by a detectable feeling of disbelief. I felt bemused on my way home; was it quite that extraordinary? And I had spoken only of the easier parts.

And as I cut down over the months, so the body became as unreliable as the mind. As the heroin dosage dropped downwards, so the consequences of slow and prolonged withdrawal became clearer. I was constantly nagged by slight sickness and at the same time the panic period, the gap which most addicts experience between junk and non-junk, was stretched unmercifully until I entered a long phase where I had the worst of both worlds, a mass of unresolved conflicts, contradictory desires resulting in negation.

For the body still wanted junk, every day and even directly after the daily, legitimate fix. The impulse was constantly to get more. Every morning now began the same way: a nightmarish interlude when I woke up, frightened and unsure where I was and why I was in pain. A run to the chemist, a quick and frustratingly small turn-on in a lavatory. Then I was left with a whole day in which to debate with myself about junk. A cold turkey might have been preferable; but I was determined to avoid short-term shock treatments with the possibility of regression, determined to cleanse the addiction once and for all.

Daily I sat trying to isolate the mechanics of junk need, observing myself, as in a laboratory. I had always conceived it as arising from a still pool. But where were the precise origins within that pool? Each day, each time the need arose, I worked backwards towards its sources. What had I been thinking of when the desire occurred? What had I been doing at the time? What common factors were there? And then, meditating. What had been the previous thoughts, just before desire had hit; what were their ramifications, leads and connections. Tracing the thoughts back in time, from the moment I had got out of bed; and in space, their associations with the rest of myself, my memory and experience. . . .

Much of the craving could be allocated to superficial levels of the organism, conditioned lines of behaviour, on the same plane as reaching for a cigarette. More of it plunged deeper into areas previously unclarified. The networks were too complex. A stage was reached every time when I could trace no further, and the trail petered out until the next attempt. Then I would be completely exhausted by the effort involved, flinging myself onto a bed to rest. But the craving would be gone, for hours at a time. Later I would retrace the steps again, identifying key points, trying to imprint paths of comprehension, the equivalent of developing new muscle tissue.

Sometimes there were no answers, or clarification was blocked, or I just got tired and disgusted with all the effort. Then I might go up to town, feeling a sense of release and escape. A large fix and temporary amnesia, heavily stoned as I had been in the first weeks of taking junk.

An unsatisfactory escape route. For the warm bath of junk lasted only until the next morning when I awoke with all the problems present again, a hangover and a craving redoubled in strength. Occasionally I scored more than one fix, perhaps a big packet of Chinese. That was worse: for the packet of stuff on the table which prior to the first turn-on would look like a roomful of gold became an oppressive threat once I had taken some, every fix representing a period of hours or days which would have to be paid for as soon as it ran out, and which would set the new pathways back again.

Most of the time I didn't score. But it was hard to see much progress yet; for I found it almost impossible to replace the positive action of going up to town with any alternative. I wanted to go; I wouldn't go—and seclusion was becoming horrible to me. It was impossible to avoid a split opening up, a schizoid fracture between the self that wanted to get junk, that represented both failure but also action, activity, communication—for stoned I would talk to anyone about anything, rambling madly—and the self that wanted to do without, passive, solitary and often hopeless.

And this battle between warring factions—as the slow attempts at integration appeared to me—had something of a science fiction quality about it, a mutant or schizophrenic in a lonely room. In tracing out all these paths of desire and illusion, just what was real any more? What parts could be considered sound? Any part of me at all?

The presence of someone close might have mitigated the worst of the self-disgust and pessimism. But I had become quite incapable of close relationships, unwilling to expose the divided mass of need and illusion which was my own image to any other human view. Short encounters with old girlfriends sometimes led to my staying the night with them, to leave, uncommunicative, the next morning, indifferent to whether they wanted to see me again or not. But I preferred the whores I had known from the West End, the structure of the transaction guaranteeing the distance I craved.

Few of these complicated reactions really surprised me, except in their intensity—after all, it was hardly new to me that trying to give up junk smashed many people. But I lacked any real faith or belief, except in my own capacity for endurance. Endurance, though, presupposed an end and I had temporarily lost sight of that end and when it might come. A perspective which I had lost and which nobody else could give me, would have told me that the despair itself was all part of the junk trap and that the greater the despair the nearer success was approaching.

I awoke with a start, darkness around me, the middle of the night, dread in my mind. Where was I, had I been dreaming? Instinctively I reached to the side of the bed for the works and the water. . . . There was no works, no water, no stuff, nothing to hold me together. . . . I slumped back on the pillows and lit a cigarette, trying to steady myself. Of course there was no junk for the middle of the night, there was no longer enough for luxuries like that.

I pulled the curtains back and stared out into the sky, trying to feel, to locate, a perspective. What was I doing here, wondering who I was? I no longer knew who the real me was, I didn't know what was real any more. Junk hardly held me together; I wasn't off, I wasn't on, I couldn't see straight, the walls were still tumbling down. Perhaps this had nothing to do with progress at all, was simply the last, sad stages of addiction, futile attempts to flee from a deteriorating organism, the brain cells crumbling. . . .

This was no good, I couldn't think at all, I was cracking up completely. I got dressed and slipped quietly out of the house. It was cold and clear outside, the air was thin and silent, the stars clustered overhead. I started walking up the hill at the back of the house, gathering myself, trying to clear my head. In the past, if I was tripped out or overdosed I would walk until the horrors disappeared, the body reasserted its balance—but now where was the balance to restore? I breathed in deeply and rhythmically, trying to assert control—and froze suddenly in the middle of my thoughts.

There was a figure, a young guy, standing under a lamp-post staring at me. Pretty face, maybe a fag. But he looked only about sixteen. And here? At this time of night? Had I seen him before, did I know that face? The boy walked towards me, coming on, stroking his hips. All right . . . I was lonely, didn't care who I slept with. But there was something unreal about this. The boy stopped; I walked towards him, staring at the old-young lascivious face—and he turned away, walked smoothly towards a tree-lined turning, looking back over his shoulder, beckoning, and was gone, split, like a puff of smoke.

I stood at the top of the road, watching, lighting a cigarette. There was no movement at all, no lights had gone on, nothing stirred but the trees in the wind. I walked down the hill slowly, looking around me carefully. Where could he have come from, to appear, like a genie, under the lamp post? The look on his face . . . my head was out of control again, adolescent fantasies rising upwards into the vacuum of my personality. A movement caught my eye, a brief flash of something under the moonlight. I walked quickly towards it—nothing there.

I went back to the house, spooked, avoiding the stars. Then I got into my brother's car, started it and gunned it up the hill, heading for the West End. I needed a break. I drove carefully, lying in wait for hallucinations, but quickly, knowing what I wanted.

Across Westminster Bridge and back into town, the river quiet in the moonlight. I parked the car behind St James' and walked up to Piccadilly, looking into the arcades and cafes for junkies.

There were none about, only the street users and hustlers and they never had anything. The Take Six. Nobody there. The lavatories. If there was anyone there they were fast asleep. I circled round Sojo, switched back on to junk time, a sense of purpose, asking one or two people I knew, a couple of whores, one junkie—but none of them had anything. Finally I stood moodily near Boots, hoping for something to turn up. The West End looked horrible, menacing, depraved. From the other side of the road, outside an arcade, a man detached himself from a group and came over to me.

'Are you looking for smack?'

I looked at him carefully, the hard appearance and a Belfast accent. You never knew who was what any more.

'No,' I said, after a pause, 'No thanks, I'm all right.'

'Someone said you were looking. What's wrong, it's good stuff.' He stank of alcohol.

'I'll be all right,' I said, walking on, I didn't like the look of the two friends who'd come across either.

But was I seeing straight? Or was I paranoid?

I walked along to Covent Garden to get a cup of coffee, avoiding the bright lights, not wishing to be seen. At the coffee stall there was the usual crowd of derelicts, porters, drunks—but no junkies. I took the cracked and steaming cup of coffee into King Street, away from the dirt and crowds, until I found a darkened doorway to sit in. I was tired. My eyes closed.

A figure in front of my face, bending over me. My eyes were clouded. More fantasy? I wasn't interested.

A knee sank into my face, slow motion, underwater. I was drowning in blood, then pain, more blows.

'The wallet, get the fucking wallet, inside.' The Belfast voice. Biology asserted itself, real or no. I covered up, lashing out, trying to get out of the doorway. The mêlée became clearer, one of them trying to hold me and get his hands in my pockets while the others hit me. Anger and self-preservation took over, seeing me to my feet, wrenching myself free of the first man, butting the second in the face, breaking loose, running along King Street, one of them grabbing at my jacket, the others following, determined but slowed by booze.

No time to decide if I was dreaming, why there was no one else in sight—as I stumbled along, reached for the doorway I had searched for, grabbed the milk bottle and brought it down in a huge sweeping arc into the side of the nearest man's face, shattering it to pieces, thrusting the remnant into his features. . . . And I ran, ran towards the river, spitting blood.

The blood was real enough.

No way back and no way forward. Dale did his best but I was almost unable to communicate even with him, and tended to answer his helpful questions with non-committal bromides. When I ducked out of his appointments the tiny scripts were sent through the post, or else the phone would ring and I knew it would be him to ask me gently if I would be turning up that evening. I told him once that I was coldly fearful of failing yet again, but that any other prospect was not in sight.

'But that's not the end of the world, I suppose,' said Dale, in his sane way. 'If you go back, you go back. There's always more junk until the next time.'

But I didn't believe in a next time. I thought of Moss and the spiral of conflict I had sought to avoid. I wondered about his feelings, alone, just before he had hanged himself with his belt, knowing finally that his time had come, that there was no way out. And all the others who had killed themselves under similar circumstances.

New Year's Day found me staring through the windows at the snow in the darkened streets outside, rooted to one spot, debating the year of my life that was gone, vanished. No way back, the way forward an unanswered question. It was taking me a long time to journey beyond fear.

15

My last prescribed fixes were in March 1971. While the worst was over by then there were no celebrations. Until the very last moment I was still clutching for something, often plucking the works out of my arm and pitching it in blind violence at the whitewashed lavatory wall, frustration at the tiny dose mingling with rage at myself for continuing to submit to the experience. Afterwards, for several months, I took small doses of oral methadone, diluting the mixture from the tap in order to cut it down to miniscule amounts, until I was free of that as well. The flames of the addiction flickered, smouldered and went out.

But freedom was a relative term and there was no sudden break or sense of liberation. Nor was there, needless to say, any one cause that could be isolated and rendered harmless. There were only the multiple threads which made up any human being and which could be slowly unravelled and retied into new patterns. The 'cure' had never run strictly in parallel with the chemical reduction, but had accompanied it, sometimes overtaking, often lagging behind.

From the darkest period, during the previous winter, a change had taken place, slowly and imperceptibly at first, gradually becoming manifest. At last I started to draw dividends from the prolonged process I had put myself through, and began to understand the magical concept of sacrifice—the translation of energy by destruction. The breakdown and disintegration had gone about as far as was possible; the mind began a building operation on the ashes. My patterns of thinking began to settle, no longer concerned with whether I was sound or not. The corrosive self-disgust disappeared and the feeling of being trapped in an unending nightmare, a sensation which, months before, had made me throw up my hands in the middle of Norwood High Street and, to the discomfort of local tradesmen, beseech the sky as to Who was writing this script—that feeling was gone.

Craving for junk recurred through the months. Sometimes I went along with it but it no longer tortured me—for I had the priceless knowledge by then of where it came from and what its limits were. My old belief, the one that had stymied me in Cane Hill—that the craving was both impossible to locate and unlikely to diminish—was shown to be incorrect.

And the map had eventually shown the way in which ideas could be converted into modes of operation. Given the effort and the resulting integration, conscious aspiration—I don't want to take junk, or other ideas—could be converted into energy. It took time and the cost was considerable, but the mechanisms were clear. The fear of failure or relapse vanished.

On the other hand I doubted if junk desire would ever go completely. The pathways of seven years would remain, dormant, emptied of most of their force but still in tenuous existence, liable to mild triggering. A familiar face, a walk down a street where I had once scored regularly, the occasional twitch in a crowd as I felt, intuitively, the presence of junk nearby—any of these and some other stimuli could set the pathways into depleted activity, the cells into a shuffle.

In practice I had to avoid the company of other addicts, for their presence and conversation was, naturally enough, the strongest stimilus of all. Perhaps in the future it might not be so, I thought; but in any case talking to junkies that I had known well was becoming a painful experience, oppressing me with thoughts of their probable fate. Seeing them from the other side of the river, especially the females, made me upset if I had been close to them, aware that the burden couldn't be shared and that there was a barrier between us.

Equally there were whole areas, geographical and social, financial and cultural, which overlapped with the junk community and which I wanted to avoid in the near future, as Terry the jazz musician had avoided the music business after leaving Cane Hill. It might have been unnecessary but I was learning caution.

Which left me out in the cold for a while. For between the 'straight' world and the areas I wanted a rest from, there was little free space. The long period of isolation and analysis coming on top of six years immersal in junk, moreover, had left me unable to see things quite the way that others saw them, straight or otherwise. After such an outside path and so much introspection, I was temporarily uninterested in the things most people had to say, preoccupied as they still seemed to be with trivia and illusion. It would pass.

Social gatherings were something of a drag, for months. Parties, reflecting as they did an alcohol-blurred and superficial way of responding to people which I had grown bored with years before, were a typical problem. After attending one or two and drinking coca cola out of respect for my socially inflexible liver, I started drinking alcohol with the rest of them. When I was sober, the sight of a roomful of people on booze was as repugnant to me as a cellar full of junkies would have been to them. But the effort was worth making.

'Who are you?' a friendly female might ask, 'what do you do?'—unaware of the force her questions could still hold for me. For a while the answers usually began: 'It's a long story. . . .' She would have done better to ask about the weather, or if I wanted to sleep with her.

I was naked once more. However, aware that the nakedness had been willed this time by myself, and also that nakedness at the age of twenty-eight had its own consolations, I was quite happy to accept it.

I had no career to return to. Writing I was uncertain about; in any case the question could wait. The need to maintain an ordinary existence resolved any debate and in the autumn I began work again, first of all casually and then—when a friend bypassed any formal interview and questions for me, slipping me in—as an office worker in the City. At least they were selling food, I thought, not pesticides.

I was certainly no worse off than someone who had just completed a prison sentence or, more appositely, returned from a war. Dropping out in the sixties meant working in the seventies. And I was in one piece, a couple of front teeth missing, some bad marks on my arms, a liver that responded to kindness and forethought—but otherwise complete.

If I had any reservations about being drawn into straight society, the alternatives could hardly be romanticized; the particular groups with which I had identified in the previous decade were scattered, their beliefs in abeyance, their members either withdrawn and temporarily defeated or looking after themselves, as I was. And the rampant individualism and anarchic belief in the self which I had espoused looked less wholesome when younger people turned it into an unsavoury and fanatical political stance.

For a while I spent my time rounding off the edges of the rebuilt personality, still influenced by some magical theories and practice. Gently I pursued the nakedness, cultivating and embracing it according to my own strange beliefs. At one time I could be found in the Kings Road, attired in curious clothes and a blond wig, arm in arm with two whores. Or I slept with guys, glorying in the loss of my past, over-rigid ego. Then I moved on. It was time to rest the head for a while. I left my brother's, moved into a flat and adopted a slightly bourgeois life style with a woman I knew.

This relaxation couldn't extend completely to junk. I kept an eye on the junk forces, as one might on a potentially dangerous dog. My ideal, no doubt, would have been to take it or leave it without complications. But that would have been a contradiction of past experience. Sometimes, still, I would decide to have a fix for the pleasure it gave. But junk wasn't hashish and didn't integrate so easily into everyday life. The period of intoxication would soon be gone, to be followed by an abominable hangover.

But junk as a way of life had become obnoxious to me. Not only were the flames of the addiction extinquished, but the belief which I had somehow managed to pour into it, the desire to hold that intangible in my hands, had also gone. And I wanted to stay as open as possible, for as long as I could, uninterested in running down the road any longer. Open, not half-closed, naked, not masked.

The case against it didn't rest on its dangers, for we all had to die and a short life-span was not—in spite of current opinion—necessarily a futile one. Nor did the weary language of psychology or social theory place it in perspective for me. I had simply developed a moral aversion to junk as a path, seeing it as a misguided attempt to deny the terms of being human.

This antipathy was no black-and-white reaction against a wasted past; I had nothing in common with the legions of young people, disappointed with their superficial exposure to junk, who gravitated to evangelism. Nor had I any views on 'abolishing' addiction, napalming the poppy fields or shooting the dealers. As always we were free to choose our tools, for better or worse. My beliefs reflected the experience as a whole. No arguments were needed against the later, destructive manifestations of junk; they never had been. It was the maze of its deceptive early power, its apparently positive qualities that needed questioning, the qualities which again and again left people without an exit by the time they realized the dangers for themselves, be they users or ex-junkies.

Junk gave a significant measure of control. Hard as it might seem to picture a junky, alone and vulnerable or violent and disorganized, as a man with control, nevertheless the mechanism existed within, the tap was plumbed into the arm. And almost every human attribute was affected by it. In return for the unpleasant difficulties which heroin brought—and the bargain had a truly Faustian edge, for real suffering lay, unseen, in the future—junkies were given the chance to organize the city within, to attain temporary dominion over the harsh problems of being human.

Some addicts would get away with it, living to a ripe old age, controlling until there was nothing left to control—or taken quickly by a painless overdose. They had my best wishes. But the escape route was for one person only at a time—those around them, the people who didn't use, would be left to fend for themselves or to pick up the pieces.

One could argue that such beliefs were superfluous, that simple common sense dictated an obvious attitude to the drug. Perhaps. But once the drug had been sampled, common sense was no longer any guide.

For myself I had no regrets, understanding the part that junk had played. But I was saddened at the fate of so many of my contemporaries. Not just because they had included many of the most gifted and original people I had known. What was upsetting was that all too often they had embarked upon the course believing it to be one of liberation. There was little sense to be made out of that, only a feeling of loss and an impression of obscure spiritual tragedy.

I didn't know what the future held. I was content to be naked, as I came in.

Glossary

Cannabis. From the plant, *cannabis sativa.* In recent years much research has been done on the drug in an attempt to locate or assess its dangers. Scientists have succeeded in isolating the active constituent, delta-9-THC, and have used it in preference to the variable normal product for their projects. Since some of their findings don't tally with everyday experience, they appear to have produced something far stronger and more threatening than the usual brand. No doubt it will find its way onto the black market and add a new chapter to the story. *Marijuana* is the drug in plant form. *Hashish* is a block concentrate made from the resin and pollen. Terms: *pot, weed, grass, hash, dope, smoke. Ganja* is another variant but is also the term used in England for West Indian cannabis. A *joint* is a cigarette containing the drug, so is a *spliff. Majoun* is a North African edible preparation. A *weight* refers to cannabis in bulk, from pounds or kilos upwards.

Cocaine. The stimulant, obtained originally from the South American coca plant. The price of progress again: the unrefined leaves are not particularly destructive. *Coke, Charlie, C. Junk* and *stuff* can include cocaine.

Heroin. Diacetylmorphine. Discovered at the turn of the century. Hopes were expressed at the time that it would be a less addictive substitute for morphine, with results that we know. *Junk, stuff, gear, smack* or *schmeck, horse, H, skag, shit* and no doubt many other terms, none of them poetic—there is a slightly obscure but significant link running through the slang. A *works* is a syringe, the needle is a *spike.* A *turn-on* is an injection or fix, but the phrase has come to be used loosely of the ingestion of other drugs. A *user* is sometimes distinguished from a *junkie,* sometimes not. A *habit* means what it says, but more so. *Stretched out, strung out,* refer to withdrawal symptoms. *Chinese* refers to illicit heroin, scored in *packets* or *bags.* The black market is no longer cornered by Chinese immigrants, but the name has tended to stick for any illicit, powdered junk. *English,* used as a noun, means the BP variety, in hypodermic tablet form.

LSD. Lysergic acid diethylamide. Hallucinogen synthesized in Switzerland during World War Two. The research chemist involved, Hoffman, was experimenting in his lab, ingested some of the drug by accident and then set out on his regular bicycle ride home. One hopes that traffic was light. *Acid.* An *acid freak* describes the regular or fanatical user, *over the edge* the frequent consequences.

Methadone. A synthetic opiate. Hopes were expressed that it would be a less addictive substitute for heroin. It is still prescribed in injectable form by clinics and is the most widely available opiate on the black market, many junkies seeking to sell it rather than use it. The money can then be used to buy heroin. It has no slang name.

Methedrine. Methylamphetamine. Strongest and most destructive of the amphetamines, the group which includes benzedrine and dexedrine. Its availability is now tightly restricted. Erstwhile users frequently switch to Ritalin, another unsavoury stimulant, the subject of some publicity a few years ago when it was given daily to small children in an American school 'because it was shown to raise their learning ability.' *Speed* is the slang term for both drugs.

Miscellaneous. Uppers are any stimulant pills. *Downers* naturally refer to the other end of the spectrum, sleeping pills—*sleepers*—or tranquillizers with a heavy, slow effect. A *speedball* is a fix of heroin and cocaine mixed, as is a *whizz-bang.* To *score* or *cop* is to obtain supplies of a drug. Being defrauded by a dealer is a *rip-off,* a *turnover* or a *mumble. Stoned, loaded, bombed out, smashed, high, out of it,* refer to various states of intoxication. *Stoned* in fact does service for them all, the degree and variety being suggested by the verbal emphasis or context. *Tripping* relates only to acid, no other drug. An *OD* is an overdose, when the slang stops.